LIZA

Her Cinderella Nightmare

Other books by James Robert Parish

Great Movie Series (*ed.*)
The Cinema of Edward G. Robinson with Alvin H. Marill

LIZA

Her Cinderella Nightmare

James Robert Parish
with Jack Ano

W. H. Allen · London
A division of Howard & Wyndham Ltd
1975

ISBN 0 491 01574 7

For Stella Pinckus

Wherever You Are

Acknowledgments

Grateful thanks go to:

Elliott Adams
Ted Albert
Linda Taylor Barnes
Nancy Barr (*Limelight for Liza*)
Louis Chaten
John Robert Cocchi
Cheri Cross
Jo Anne Darzin
Ernest Dobbs
Michael B. Druxman
Betty Ellsworth
Olivier Eyquem
Ferncliff Cemetery (V. E. Angerole)
Film Facts (Ernest Parmentier)
Films in Review
David Finkle
Focus on Films
Ethel Geisinger
Fred Guidry
Pierre Guinle
Mrs John Henning
Edward Holtzmann
Richard M. Hudson
Lloyd Ibert
Lois Kibbee
Jane and Steve Klain
Don Koll
Marvin A. Krauss
Davis S. Landay
Ernest Leogrande
Betty and Hilton Levy
Paige Lucas
Edward O. Lutz
Jack Lyons
David McGillivray
Albert B. Manski
Alvin H. Marill
Mrs Earl Meisinger
Jim Meyer

Peter Miglierini
Lynn Montgomery
Monthly Film Bulletin
Michael R. Pitts
Grace Riefner
Randie Riefner
Sal Rosa
Carol Roth
Mr and Mrs Harold Roth
Mel Schuster

Screen Facts (Alan G. Barbour)
Florence Solomon
James Spada
Don E. Stanke
Thomas E. Steinfeld
Charles K. Stumpf
Nora Taylor
Lou Valentino
Steven Whitney

and special thanks to Paul Myers, curator of the Theatre Collection at the Lincoln Centre Library for the Performing Arts, and his staff: Monty Arnold, David Bartholomew, Rod Bladel, Donald Fowle, Maxwell Silverman, Dorothy Swerdlove, Betty Wharton, and Don Madison of photographic services.

CHAPTER ONE

The world was in mourning but Liza wanted to be gay. In fact, she insisted on it. The occasion had to be 'bright and lovely', and Liza knew that, under the circumstances, this would not be easy.

Judy Garland, the forty-seven-year-old queen of the comebacks, was giving her final show at Frank E. Campbell's fashionable Manhattan upper East Side funeral home. This showcase followed a public viewing by an estimated twenty-one thousand fans and curiosity seekers, mobs of whom had been milling about all week long so as not to be denied a place of proximity at the final rites.

The greyness of that Friday afternoon in June, 1969, somehow accentuated the already grotesque aura as the shrieking hordes surged around the imposing funeral home at Madison Avenue and 81st Street like dress extras from the public execution sequences in *A Tale of Two Cities*. Their big, unrehearsed scene came just before the private services, when some people broke through police barricades to grab at the glamorous and once glamorous personalities in attendance. In the occasional tasteless moment, some fans would brazenly demand identification from figures once famous but now generally forgotten, such as middle-aged Freddie Bartholomew who, in 1938, had starred with Judy in *Listen, Darling* at MGM.

Most of the assemblage, though, was content to remain behind barriers and gape at the flow of celebrities. It was, after all, a genuine superstar event with Katharine Hepburn, Cary Grant, Frank Sinatra, Burt Lancaster, Jack Benny, Dean Martin, Lana Turner, Lauren Bacall, Sammy Davis Jnr, Ray Bolger and, of course, pint-sized Mickey Rooney at their movie-star best: the ladies adorned in brightly patterned cottons or Gucci prints with matching accessories, the men resplendent in blazers or mod suits.

They had come to pay their final respects to Judy as she would have wanted it, and Liza now wished it: with an upbeat of warmth.

On the outside, as far as the public was concerned on that summery day, Judy was going out in style, and even on the inside among the personalities present there could have been few then aware that as one legend lay embalmed another was being created . . . the legend of one Liza Minnelli.

It had not been planned that way. Judy's husband of three months, Mickey Deans, seemed, in the opinion of some observers, stunned and unable to cope with his special duties as Mr Judy Garland number five-and-last. Someone had to take charge and that responsibility fell to Liza Minnelli, age twenty-three, Judy's 'ugly duckling' first-born and the one person close to Garland who probably was least in her debt.

Long in Garland's shadow, Liza had emerged in the final years of her mother's tumultuous life as a daughter of whom she could be justifiably proud and also as a performer who might some day be her fiercest rival. Garland, not surprisingly, was the first fully to recognise the extraordinary potential in her talented daughter. During their joint appearance at the London Palladium in 1964, she made it clear, if briefly, that there was room for only one 'living legend' in the family—and that Judy was it!

Now the great star was dead and already Liza's own star was rising to fill the void left by her late mother. It was an irony that jaded Judy herself would have probably found amusing. The competition Judy had feared from fledgling Liza could no longer be checked. As producer and director of the Judy Garland funeral, Liza Minnelli also became its undisputed star.

Obviously, it was a very difficult time for Liza and the complex situation was not made easier by the terms of her mother's will. Judy had wanted a cheerful and unpretentious funeral that would be followed by cremation. She left specific, detailed instructions for make-up, burial dress and even casket specifications.

Liza, as if to prove to the world and herself that the bonds between mother and daughter had never been broken (or seriously challenged), determined that all would be just as Judy desired it.

Liza would please Mama one more time.

CHAPTER TWO

Liza was spending the weekend at Southampton on Long Island, preparing her role in *Tell Me That You Love Me, Junie Moon*, the Otto Preminger–Paramount feature film then in pre-production, when she received *the* call from her secretary, Deanna Wenble.

It had happened that morning, Sunday, June 22nd, in London, at Judy's small honeymoon cottage in Cadogan Lane. As Mickey Deans would recall it soon afterwards in a mock-lurid article for *Look* magazine, he had smashed into the smallish, locked bathroom to find his bride naked, straddled on the toilet seat. Even as he clutched at the stiffened and contorted figure, he knew it was already too late.

'I picked her up and blood came from her nose and mouth,' Deans wrote. 'The air escaping from her mouth sounded like a low moan.'

The assumption that spread quickly throughout the world was that Judy was a suicide victim. Deans seemed too removed from reality by shock and grief to offer convincing denials.

Liza, however, was in quick command of the situation. She responded, courageously and without outward show of emotion, the way Junie Moon, of the forthcoming Preminger film, might have behaved in such a situation. She would not allow production of the Paramount film to be delayed, despite the director's willingness to do so, and she refused to take time off from the already crowded work schedule.

Dealing methodically with each facet of the calamity, she first had to contend with the gaggle of sensation-seeking reporters. She informed them, 'It wasn't suicide, it wasn't sleeping pills, it wasn't cirrhosis.' This trans-Atlantic prognostication was made by Liza before the release of the official British coroner's report which listed Judy's death as accidental due to 'incautious self-overdosage' of the barbiturate, Seconal.

'My mother had that wild impatient streak to live,' Liza told the press in statements that were to be repeated by James Mason, Judy's co-star in *A Star Is Born*, at the funeral eulogy.

'It was her love of life that carried her through everything,' she explained. 'The middle of the road was never for her. It bored her. She wanted the pinnacle of excitement. If she was happy, she wasn't just happy—she was ecstatic. And when she was sad, she was sadder than anybody.

'She had lived eighty lives in one,' the star's first-born continued, 'and yet I thought she would outlive us all. She was a great star and a great talent and for the rest of my life I will be proud to be Judy Garland's daughter.'

Funeral arrangements, even under the simplest circumstances, are a tense, trying business. Liza surprised everyone, including herself, by the dispatch with which she handled the chores at hand.

When Mickey Deans had spoken with Liza he had asked her if they should follow through with Judy's own request, spoken in a moment of premonition some months before in England: 'Mickey, if anything happens to me, take me home.'

Liza relayed to the London-based Deans the fact that Sid Luft, Judy's husband number three, had already telephoned her from California. He had wanted Judy buried in California, but Liza said to Mickey on the trans-Atlantic phone connection, 'Mama hated California.' So it was agreed to bury Judy in New York with the funeral services and viewing to be held at the 'Final Showplace of the Stars,' the Frank E. Campbell Funeral Home.

Some rumour collectors have insisted that when Luft did not win his way about a California burial, he tossed out the wild notion that Judy be interned above 'the showplace of the nation' in the conveniently named Rainbow Room of Rockefeller Centre. But Liza was not about to have the funeral transformed into the kind of three-ring circus that would see Judy being sent off with something approaching twilight services at Radio City Music Hall. She could not prevent the public's final goodbye to Judy being hysterical on their part, but she intended to give the occasion as much dignity as she could muster and arrange.

While Judy's body was at Westminster Hospital in London for the autopsy preceding the inquest on Wednesday, June 25th, Liza, back in New York, was completing the funeral arrangements and making additional statements to the demanding press. She was helped in this nerve-racking period by her god-mother-mentor Kay Thompson, whom Liza had manoeuvred into the *Junie Moon* cast as Miss Gregory, the rich, eccentric landlady.

When the plane carrying Deans and the corpse of Garland arrived at Kennedy Airport on June 26th just past midnight, Liza was there with Kay Thompson. It was a gruesome 'reunion' for mother and daughter. It was the type of traumatic scene that not even the slickest television soap-opera writer could do full justice to, for neither the late Judy nor the quivering, living Liza were ordinary persons in any sense of the words.

Later, when it came time to pick a coffin, and a small mahogany one was selected, Liza blurted out, 'But it must be white.' No sooner did the Frank Campbell's director tell her that they had none available in white, than Kay Thompson shot forth with, 'At MGM we'd get a spray gun and paint it white.' It seemed a practical solution to following Liza's and Judy's dictates.

It was Liza who demanded that the whitened casket be covered with glass to prevent any attempt at desecration by fans and grasping memento seekers. It was Liza who decided that the funeral should be carried through in a theme of yellow and white, and it was she who ordered a full blanket of yellow roses to be draped around Judy's coffin, with an additional spray of yellow and white chrysanthemums. It would also be Liza, following Judy's wishes, who requested that no one attending the funeral wear black.

Protests from widower Deans kept Liza from observing her mother's request for cremation, and the action of Eva ('I-am-a-star') Gabor prohibited cosmetics man Gene Hibbs from being in attendance to follow Judy's wishes and do her make-up as he had on all her MGM movies. It seemed that the Hungarian personality, who was being featured in the *Green Acres* television series, had Hibbs under exclusive contract and she was unable to forgo his professional attentions for even a day.

The funeral service on Friday afternoon the 27th took approximately forty minutes. James Mason flew in from Switzerland to deliver the eulogy, which began: 'The thing about Judy Garland was that she was so alive. . . .' The Reverend Peter Delaney, who had known Judy and Mickey Deans in London and had, in fact, blessed the couple following their wedding, concluded the service with a reading from I Corinthians, chapter thirteen, verses one to thirteen.

Thereafter, Judy's body was taken to Ferncliff Cemetery in Hartsdale, some few minutes from Scarsdale where Liza had gone to school and Judy had resided off and on in 1961. The coffin was placed in a temporary vault in the Ferncliff Mausoleum. In deciding upon permanent arrangements there, the family agreed to wait until a new addition—then under construction—was completed. It would be Liza who would eventually pay for Judy's internment in this new crypt section on November 4th, 1970. The inscription on the front of the Italian marble-faced crypt (measuring 3 × 3 × 9 feet) would read 'JUDY GARLAND 1922—1969'. According to the Ferncliff Cemetery Association, no provisions have been made yet for other members of Judy's family.

When Deans, the Reverend Peter Delaney, and a

few others returned from the cemetery, they went directly to Liza's East Side apartment where Kay Thompson had prepared food, drink, and a few appropriate wisecracks hopefully to cheer up the morose gathering. Then, after bewildered Joey Luft, Judy's third and last-born, had been put to bed, the group decided to visit a mutual acquaintance in New Jersey. During the glum car ride to Jersey, they happened to turn on the radio and one music station was broadcasting Judy's Carnegie Hall concert. Judy's strong voice could be heard singing *The Man that Got Away.*

It was Liza, according to Deans in his book *Weep No More, My Lady*, who begged them to 'leave it on'. The car passengers listened in silence, and then suddenly, it was Liza who shouted out, 'Go, Mama, go!'

CHAPTER THREE

She was a child of the gods—or at least that is the way the supreme power at Metro-Goldwyn-Mayer regarded the Piscean birth of Liza May Minnelli at Cedars of Lebanon Hospital in Hollywood on Tuesday, March 12th, 1946.

Louis B. Mayer liked to boast that he had under contract 'more stars than there are in heaven' and, at the time, there was no star in the MGM celluloid galaxy bigger than diminutive (4' 11", 7 stones 7 pounds) Judy Garland. Though Judy was a magical box-office name and a million-dollar commodity for the expansive studio, it was Liza's father who most impressed mogul Mayer.

The son of an Italian violinist and a French opera singer, Vincente Minnelli was born on February 28th in Chicago some time after 1900. While some sources insist it was 1913, Liza once told reporters, 'No one knows his real age. He even lied on my birth certificate.'

He debuted at the age of three in the Minnelli Brothers tent shows and, as an adult, found employment as a stage manager and costume designer before coming to New York. In Manhattan he served as art director and co-ordinating director for stage presentations at New York film theatres. Then, in 1933, he was appointed art director at Radio City Music Hall. After some time as a Broadway producer (*At Home Abroad*, *Ziegfeld Follies*, *Very Warm for May*, *The Show Is On*, *Hooray for What*) he went to MGM in 1940 as a master of all trades: story editor, writer, designer, and director of special sequences. Finally, in 1943, he was entrusted with a feature film: the stringently-budgeted adaptation of the Broadway musical, *Cabin in the Sky*, with an all-black cast headed by Ethel Waters, Lena Horne, Eddie 'Rochester' Anderson, and Louis Armstrong. Though the film was not expected to get many play dates outside what was then considered the 'sepia' market, critical enthusiasm for the performers and for Minnelli's boldly innovative directorial style helped it penetrate beyond its intended areas, and it achieved a modest 'sleeper' success.

Mayer was impressed, but not really convinced that Minnelli's flash of success was anything more than a fluke. His next assignment was another minor picture, *I Dood It*, starring the fading dancer Eleanor Powell, rising B picture comic Red Skelton, and guest appearances by Lena Horne and organist Ethel Smith. The 102-minute black-and-white feature surprisingly proved to be one of 1943's bigger hits and Minnelli immediately graduated to what Mayer considered a most important and difficult screen project,

Arthur Freed's production of *Meet Me in St Louis* (1944).

It was the kind of homey, Technicolor, escapist movie that only MGM would have considered making in wartime. Even at this most powerful of studios, the planned production held uncommon risks. It was to be a musical in which the songs would realistically advance, rather than merely embellish, the frail story-line. Though the Metro picture would have the star power of Judy Garland, supported by the popular Margaret O'Brien, Judy was an unwilling participant and the strains of her off-camera life were beginning to take their enormous tolls both physically and emotionally.

Judy's so-called 1941 'elopement' with studio musician-composer David Rose (who had divorced Martha Raye for Judy), in which they were accompanied by her mother on their Las Vegas honeymoon, had roused Mayer's ire, and it was later alleged by the star that he did everything to ensure the failure of the union. By the time *Meet Me in St Louis* began production, the marriage survived in name only and Judy was a high-strung, sometimes hysterical girl dangerously close to mental collapse.

Mayer's attempted solution to Judy's mounting problems was a continuation of policies long practised. His favourite doctor supervised Judy's tortuous diets and plied the star with a variety of pills to keep her docile at one moment and dramatically alert the very next. In recognition of her emotional disturbances, and in a successful manœuvre to keep her from seeking more reliable psychological counsel that could not be controlled, he sent her to a series of studio-monitored psychiatrists who would control her insecurities with therapies literally prescribed to keep her from becoming overly temperamental on the set.

Minnelli's directorial status on *Meet Me in St Louis* offered further insurance against the star's potential misbehaviour. A kindly and gentle man off the sound stage, he was known as a martinet among directors and, at first, Judy found him an impossibly hard taskmaster.

She resented the role of Esther Smith because she considered it adolescent and bland, another 'Dorothy Adorable' characterisation extending from her *The Wizard of Oz* image, and she believed that she was now ready for more dramatic adult roles. But she was under contract and final decisions were made by the studio executives. She was a professional and she would give what she considered her best.

Minnelli, however, was not satisfied and he demanded more than Judy was initially prepared to offer. On the first day of shooting, he ordered twenty-five takes on a sequence the star considered a minor episode within the film. She resorted to tears but Minnelli seemed unmoved. She would do the scene until she got it the way he wanted. Gradually, Judy realised that he was drawing from her acting, singing, and dancing resources that had not previously been revealed on screen and by the time the picture was completed she and Minnelli were living together.

Their initial liaison, however, was brief. Minnelli's autocratic strength on the sound stages did not extend to his private life and, at this time of her life, the twenty-one-year-old Judy was in search of a man who could be both father and lover. Soon they parted and she drifted back to the brilliantly acerbic writer Joseph L. Mankiewicz (soon to become the well-known director of such adult films as *A Letter to Three Wives* and *All about Eve*), who had been fired by Mayer when he tried to lead Judy to more reputable psychiatric treatment than she had been receiving under studio auspices. She also found comfort with composer David Raksin who wrote for her a melody that he called *Judy*, but which became better known when adapted as the title song for Otto Preminger's movie, *Laura* (1944).

It was inevitable in the cloistered environment 'behind the wall' at MGM that Minnelli and Judy would be drawn together again.

Imperious Greer Garson was having difficulties achieving a musical self-parody in 'The Great Lady Has an Interview' sequence for Minnelli's all-star spectacle *Ziegfeld Follies* (filmed in 1944 but not released until 1946), and Judy was soon brought in to replace her. Again, Vincente revealed new facets of her performing artistry, most notably a bedazzling flair for sophisticated comedy that would never again be successfully utilised by Judy on screen despite Minnelli's attempt in the ill-fated *The Pirate* in 1948. Soon, in an unprecedented display of star authority, Judy was demanding that Minnelli replace Fred Zinnemann as director of *The Clock* (1945), a much-plagued project that was especially important to the star because it afforded her a rare opportunity as an adult dramatic actress.

Judy's faith in Minnelli was not misplaced. Her motion pictures with him have withstood the test of time, a fact which applies to few of her other feature-films.

Looking back at her heritage, Liza once remarked, 'Bette Davis recently told me that the first musical in which kids weren't getting ready to put on a show in a barn was a simple story of an American family called *Meet Me in St Louis*. She said the first version of *Love Story* was about two people meeting and marrying during a weekend in World War II. That was *The Clock*.'

It was during the production of *The Clock*, which co-starred Robert Walker, that Judy and Minnelli began living together again. They soon determined to wed.

The marriage took place on June 15th, 1945, exactly one week after the granting of her divorce from David Rose. Ira Gershwin was Minnelli's best man and Betty Asher, Judy's publicist and long-time friend, was bridesmaid. Louis B. Mayer, substituting for Judy's long deceased father, proudly gave the bride away.

During the Minnellis' extended New York honeymoon, Judy learned that she was pregnant.

The months that followed were the happiest the newlyweds were to share. After shooting her brief sequences in *Till the Clouds Roll By* (1946) as Marilyn Miller singing *Look for the Silver Lining* and *Who*, Judy went into retirement to await the birth of her child and Minnelli began work on *Undercurrent* (1946) with Katharine Hepburn, Robert Taylor, and Robert Mitchum.

It was a time of relaxation and the experience was new for Judy. She abandoned the pills upon which she had become so dependent and she played at being a 'normal' housewife: scrubbing floors, cooking, and attempting to sew with blithe disregard for the battalion of servants at her command.

The baby, she decided, would be called Vincente, Jnr, if a boy and Liza, after the Gershwin song and in tribute to lyricist Ira, if a girl. Because of Judy's narrow pelvis, a Caesarian birth was suggested and Tuesday, March 12th, was selected as the date of delivery. Judy's anticipation and happiness overwhelmed any uncertainties or fears. 'Tuesday's child is full of joy' . . . nothing could go wrong. She would have a perfect baby.

And that is how the parents saw the birth. Minnelli, writing of his daughter, said, 'She was, of course, the most beautiful baby in the nursery. There, alone on a table, was a perfect child, with absolutely no wrinkles.'

Others would not always concur in the proud father's assessment of his child's beauty, for her features, then as now, seemed to accentuate the most pronounced characteristics of each parent. Liza, herself, has always doubted her physical attractiveness and, on one occasion, says she came 'within minutes' of having her nose bobbed.

'There's some people that can't keep their clothes on because they have really pretty bodies, but I'm just embarrassed,' she has said. 'If I were thin and looked really swell, maybe I wouldn't be embarrassed but when I was little I was always pudgy and it stayed with me. The fact is that I'm just embarrassed, that's all.'

Thomas Thompson of *Life* magazine, while thoroughly in admiration of her as an extraordinary talent and personality, wrote that the grown-up Liza looked as if '. . . the parts might have been assembled by a weary parent on Christmas Eve'.

Thompson went on to muse how '. . . if the eyes are too big, and they are twice too big, and if they surround a nose that could be subdivided . . . and if the teeth are borrowed from a rabbit soliciting carrots, and if the voice could summon sentry dogs, and if she does not walk so much as lurch, glide and jerk in continuing peril of collapsing like a rag doll dismissed by a bored child . . . how can this girl put together in the Flea Market, how can Liza Minnelli, at twenty-three, possibly threaten to become the major entertainment figure that she is becoming?'

CHAPTER FOUR

A lot of myths have arisen concerning Liza's childhood, many of them perpetrated by Liza herself who, in the early stages of her career, generally bypassed truth in favour of the colourful, if innocuous stories that could be embroidered into a suitable tapestry of her life.

Her actions are not without logic. Early in life she had learned that the press all too frequently advances itself or its publications at the expense of the public personality. If not even the *New York Times* would print the truth when it was offered to it, as it was by respected writers like Tom Burke, then Liza reasonably believed that she could attempt to control the invasion into the privacy of herself and her family by creating personally the fictions she believed would make good copy.

There was one basic flaw in her reasoning. When the press became aware of the deceit, one that had been diligently practised also by Judy Garland in the later years of her life, it then felt free to invent and report as fact the most outlandish of fabricated stories concerning the newsworthy Liza. Unwittingly, she had provided the public media with the fuel upon which to ignite the flames of notoriety.

Though Liza has continued to be extremely wary of the press and, especially, of would-be biographers, she has in recent times become more honest in dealing with the fourth estate. In addition, she has been especially revealing in television and radio interviews where, despite the editings made possible by the predominance of taped live broadcasts, she can be assured that some semblance of her actual statements will survive.

'I had the best life,' Liza told ace columnist Rona Barrett in a taped interview a few years ago. 'I really had a weird life but I really had a great life. . . . We laughed, you know. Nobody wants to hear about that.'

It was unlikely that no one wanted to know about the good times that were evolving out of the unhappiest of circumstances. However, to have laughed at the misfortunes that were constantly befalling Judy Garland and her family throughout the post-World War II decades would have seemed to most of the public an exhibition of insensitivity. Much of the entertainment public had learned to accept black comedy in the fictions of Vladimir Nabokov and Terry Southern, but not in real life—and certainly not concerning vulnerable Judy Garland. If she could not for ever be the perfect epitome of the all-American girl next door, then in the demanding and sometimes hypocritical minds of her fans, she must become a figure of tragedy.

Judy accepted the role foisted on her by the 'adoring' public, believing most of the time that it was only a part. Nevertheless, she played it to the hilt. She began tailoring her stage performances to fit the new mould without ever forgetting the old, making herself into the American Edith Piaf, the helpless sparrow seeking eternal flight 'over the rainbow'. And she made it work magnificently.

'Sympathy is my business,' she proudly told Liza in what was to be just one of many lessons on how, in atmospheres of fantasy such as theirs, one must quickly learn to distinguish between what is real and what is fake. Liza learned the lesson well, but, at the age of nineteen, she added an amendment of her own drawn from personal experience. 'I know some people who think reality must be constantly depressing, but I think reality is something you rise above.'

Reality, though, is seldom far from Liza's mind. 'I don't have dreams of white picket fences any more,' she told Miss Rona, 'because I found out they're uncomfortable to sit on.'

Judy taught her impressionable daughter with bluntness and thoroughness. 'I'm your best example of what not to do,' she urged and Liza has followed the advice whenever her shifting coterie of supporters allows and when she has the fortitude to remember. In warning her daughter, then a teenager, of the vulnerability of the famous, Judy offered a macabrely comic consolation borrowed from James Jones' novel, *From Here to Eternity*: 'They may kill us, but they'll never eat us.'

It was, as Liza admits, a weird life, but it was also an enormously rich and privileged one. She was especi-

20

ally fortunate in having parents of enormous complexity and talent who, if not always compatible with each other, none the less gave their daughter the complementary virtues and weaknesses that have been responsible for Liza's rare qualities as both a person and a performer.

Vincente Minnelli is a man of undisputed culture and outward sensitivity, a figure of presumed confidence and calm in even the stormiest of situations, and he is one of the major creative forces in the annals of motion pictures. From him, Liza must have inherited the extraordinary taste and instinct that enable her to surround herself professionally with talents of the very highest order, often, as in the case of Oscar-winning composer-musical arranger Marvin Hamlisch, long before their abilities are generally recognised. From Minnelli, too, Liza must have received the rhythmic grace which makes her dancing at least as exciting as her work as a singer. Above all, it is to him that she owes her exuding Latin warmth: the need to touch and be touched and to make of each friendship a long-lasting relationship.

Judy bestowed equally valuable qualities on her now globally acclaimed daughter. There are the obvious traits: the nervous energy, the coltish laugh, the singing voice filled with *vibrato* that seems to echo generations of 'born in a trunk/the show must go on' traditions, and the innate theatricality.

But it is to Judy, also, that Liza probably owes her physical strength, her drive, and her determination. When not befuddled by the amphetamines and barbiturates to which she had unwillingly and unwittingly become addicted by studio prescription, Judy was a woman of essential sanity and enormous strength. Only a person of uncommon strength and will could have survived as long as she did.

But Judy not only survived for a long period, she also enjoyed turning her life into an extended run of black comedy in her surviving. From her mother, Liza obtained her macabre sense of humour, an acceptance of injustice and the ability to fight back *only* when it was and is important to win. Directly and indirectly from the evidence of Judy's experience and intentions, Liza achieved a worldly-wise but never world-weary wisdom.

It was a rich heritage, rich enough to sustain Liza through the monstrously difficult early years. Like her mother, she would find humour in the most bizarre of situations and, desperately seeking love and attention, she would clown energetically in a manner that would inspire her godmother, the ever-turbaned Kay Thompson (born in St Louis in 1912), to base her celebrated *Eloise* stories on Liza's juvenile pranks.

At other times, Liza's feeling of insecurity would literally overwhelm her and she would be afraid to make her presence known. One of her earliest memories was of frequently being allowed to sleep with her parents. 'They'd put me in the middle and we'd all go to sleep,' Liza revealed in an 'as told to Muriel Davidson' article in *Good Housekeeping*, 'but sometimes during the night, in their sleep, they'd hold hands across my stomach or my head. I didn't dare move for fear I'd get tossed out. I didn't want that because it was so warm and dark and safe there.'

Though neither parent was then willing to admit it, even privately, Liza had been born into a troubled home environment that was to worsen drastically in the early months of her life.

Judy was making *The Pirate* (1948) under Minnelli's direction at MGM and it had all the potential markings of a box-office blockbuster. There was Gene Kelly to co-star, plus an original score by Cole Porter, a strong satiric script drawn from a play by S. N. Behrman that had starred the Lunts on Broadway, and it was planned that Liza would make her professional debut in a bit role in this Technicolor feature.

Liza was at the studio during pre-production costume fittings and she was dutifully photographed with her parents, but the on-screen appearance never materialised. *The Pirate* became a nightmare for Judy (who had become painfully thin and seemed to be existing on nervous energy alone) and Vincente, and an embarrassment to MGM executives, who reiterated their 'I told you so' doubts about allowing Judy and Kelly to appear contra-image in a sophisticated musical comedy. In production for nearly a year, the film was withheld from release until 1948 when it was felt that Judy had made a sufficiently good comeback in the more conventional *Easter Parade* (1948) to withstand the inevitable failure of *The Pirate*. The two motion pictures were released less than a month apart. *The Pirate*, despite some enthusiastic critical comment and a face-saving opening at the plush Radio City Music Hall, was shunted mainly into second-rate twin bill bookings, and *Easter Parade* was distributed to the more prestigious cinemas.

Judy had begun *The Pirate* in a jubilant, if false sense of well-being that was quickly shattered. She thought this film would provide her with an excellent opportunity to play polished comedy and she had worked well with Gene Kelly in *For Me and My Gal* (1942). Even more importantly, she believed that it would strengthen the bond between herself and Minnelli. Her confidence this time was misplaced.

Minnelli, in his autobiography *I Remember It Well* (1974), says he now realises that, with Gene Kelly in *The Pirate*, he became involved in what he calls '. . . the most intense professional association I had ever had with an actor'. Hurt and bewildered and believing, too, that Vincente was tailoring the picture to Kelly's specific talents at her expense, Judy became violently jealous and turned once again to pills and alcohol. Make-up could not disguise her day-to-day deterioration.

She found each session on the Metro sound stages a nightmare and her behaviour, according to Minnelli, turned into that of a paranoiac. Tragically, too, the cameras captured her nervousness and hostility. As the production dragged on, with retake after retake demanded for the now often hysterical Judy, she found herself unable to face the 'evil eye' and she was often absent from the set. So traumatic was the experience that Judy would never again face the motion picture cameras with ease.

At home, at night, with Vincente, matters were no better. Both parents lavished love on Liza, probably in unconscious competition with each other, but the child was exposed also to the long silences between them and to their loud, angry, and very frequent quarrels.

A few days after *The Pirate* was finally completed, on July 10, 1947, Judy entered a private sanatorium in Los Angeles. Liza, then fourteen months old, was allowed to visit her emotionally ailing mama.

After she came home from the sanatorium, Judy and Vincente each made a concerted effort to patch their stormy marriage and, for a time, it seemed to be working. Judy was reluctant, however, to start work on her next film. Her fears were understandable since it was to be MGM's *Easter Parade* with Minnelli as director and Gene Kelly again cast opposite her.

Minnelli was casting the supporting roles in *Easter Parade* when producer Arthur Freed summoned him. Judy's psychiatrists wisely felt that he should be removed from the picture and replaced by, say, Charles Walters, for it was the doctor's belief that Minnelli symbolised to Judy her troubles at the studio. The switch was made and then Kelly, supposedly having broken his ankle during dance rehearsal, was in turn replaced by Fred Astaire. Fortuitously *Easter Parade* emerged as a glowing tribute to the ebullient, if unimaginative, type of sugary musical that the studio could so cagily deliver to the accepting public. Its popularity put Judy right back on top of the screen star heap.

Through all the *Easter Parade* turmoils, Judy's marriage survived with Liza as its centre. The Minnellis tried to give their daughter what they considered a 'normal' home life. She ate with them, often slept with them, but by now it was becoming apparent that the upheavals in the Minnelli household had not left Liza unscathed. Liza demanded love. She insisted not only on attention—but on being the *centre* of attention.

At one of her early birthday parties, Minnelli

25

momentarily ignored his daughter to talk with some of the other young guests. It was Liza's occasion, her party and she was not going to be deprived of her glory. Violently, she began pounding and slapping her father with her fists and palms. Years later, when appearing at the London Palladium with her mother in Judy's show, she would discover the other side of the coin, somewhat more subtly, when Garland, jealous of the attentions Liza was receiving from *her* audience, literally shoved her daughter off stage.

By the age of two, Liza was a competent swimmer (one of the benefits of having a pool in the back yard), and she could manœuvre home ground on all fours as if on ball-bearings but she had not yet begun to stand by herself. One day, a guest shamed the child by drawing attention to a boy six months younger who was scampering about on his legs. Liza fixed woman and boy with hostile glares. The next day she walked.

Two of the more 'telling' episodes in young Liza's life would be constantly played up as major events when later retold in the fan magazines. Each new chronicler of the girl's VIP life would elaborate on the tales, drawing more and more far-reaching psychological conclusions from the apparently isolated events.

The first occurred when Vincente returned from the studio one day and, by way of conversation with Liza, made some reference to an event at the home lot that was commanding his major attention. Little Liza wheeled about and ran through the house in search of Judy. She trotted from room to room, insistent on finding her Mama. She finally located Judy at poolside and breathlessly exclaimed that Daddy—at long last—had finally talked *to* her.

The other episode could have been a scene yanked from *Meet Me in St Louis*. It was Halloween time and Liza was to be allowed to dress in costume and then to make the rounds of the neighbourhood homes in the company of her protective father. After much discussion, it was decided she could go in a witch's outfit, one adapted from Mama's *The Wizard of Oz*. Vincente devoted much effort to duplicating each bit of clothing for the ensemble to fit petite Liza, and even supervised her make-up. Then father and daughter proceeded out into the early evening. At each house, Liza was convinced that with her disguise none of the neighbours could or would recognise her. But the same routine occurred at mansion after mansion: she would excitedly ring the doorbell, the door would open, and the house owner would casually say, 'Oh hello, Liza' and give her some treats for her goodie bag. Then Minnelli led his determined youngster to the Gene Kelly abode. Much to her delight when the door opened and Kelly greeted them, he jumped back in mock terror and even began climbing the walls. Liza screamed with glee. Her daddy had created a successful occasion for her.

It was during these early years that Liza started becoming accustomed to frequent separations from her mother. Judy's psychiatrist presumably felt it would be best if she could sometimes get away by herself and away, too, from the Minnelli home which Vincente loved and Judy openly professed to hate. A second house was rented in the Hollywood hills and, for a while, the family would alternate living in the two homes. Soon, however, the squabbling Minnellis were periodically using them as separate residences and, on these increasingly more frequent occasions, Liza would remain with Vincente.

Inevitably, the time would come when the child would be separated from both parents. Liza was three and she regards the experience as 'my first horrendous recollection'.

She knew her mother had to go away. She did not know why, but she had become accustomed to Judy's periodic absences and was not particularly disturbed by the imminent departure. Liza and Vincente accompanied Judy to the train, but at the time of departure, Judy became hysterical and unconsolable. She was going away for ever, she believed. She would never return. The child observed all this with mounting fear. Could this be really happening? She tugged at her parents, sought their embrace, and then had to watch helplessly as Minnelli boarded the train with her mother, saying that he must accompany her. He could not leave Judy alone now.

'I sobbed and screamed to be taken too,' recalls Liza, 'but all I could do was stand there and watch the train pull away.' A chauffeur and nanny took the child home.

Judy was away for twelve weeks, supposedly having a 'rest cure' at a private hospital in Boston. Actually, she was withdrawing from drugs. She had been fired recently from the production of *Annie Get Your Gun*— Paramount's Betty Hutton replaced her in this 1950 musical—and she had started losing her hair. Neither she nor Minnelli had realised, they maintained, that the 'respectable' pills prescribed to her by studio doctors were actually more addictive and toxic than opiates and that her erratic behaviour had been caused by the drugs and not by what Minnelli had termed 'mental phantoms'.

Liza, meanwhile, was having her first experience in self-pity. When Minnelli returned three days later, he brought his daughter a toy drum. 'I beat it until it fell apart,' Liza recalls, 'and when Mama came home, I threw the drum away.'

However, not all of Liza's early life was unpleasant or psychologically disturbing. Much of it was positively magical for she was growing up in an atmosphere which would seem a wonderland to any child: the sound stages and back lots at MGM which Liza regarded as playground, backyard, and the place where you learned about really interesting things after school was over.

Her first real experience on a sound stage was also her screen debut, appearing with her mother and Van Johnson in the final sequence of *In the Good Old Summertime* (1949). Not quite three years old, Liza was required only to toddle along with her on camera parents and to smile prettily. On screen, however, she seemed embarrassed, frightened, and fidgety. With good reason. Liza had insisted upon dressing herself in a frilly white outfit for the scene and she was not aware until Johnson lifted her in his arms and she felt his cold hand underneath her that she had forgotten her panties.

Her next public appearance offered further evidence that Liza would never replace Margaret O'Brien or Jackie 'Butch' Jenkins as MGM's leading child star. This appearance was in a school play. Liza was five

29

and was given the important role of the Virgin Mary. As her parents proudly watched, Liza came to stage centre holding the doll that represented the baby Jesus. 'I dropped the kid,' confesses Liza.

Barring a brief bit in Minnelli's 1954 movie, *The Long, Long Trailer*, ten years would pass before Liza's next, more successful comeback attempt. Her failures as an actress did not keep young Liza from the Metro lot, however, where, because of the prominent positions held by her parents, she was accorded the courtesies usually attendant only to visiting princesses. She rode on the camera booms with her father and she had open access to sets and rehearsal halls. No one knew where to expect her next, for Liza had quickly investigated and mastered all the underground passage ways, short cuts, and 'secret' executive entrances to the sets and sound stages. Most often, though, she could be found, even when Garland or Minnelli were working elsewhere, in rehearsal halls B or C watching the studio dancers perfecting their intricate routines.

If Liza was a princess at the studio, she was a queen at home and she ruled over all the wealthy neighbourhood children in an environment that close friend Candice Bergen now recognises as being '. . . on the highest level of the absurd . . . all highly surrealistic, like living in a big playroom'.

Though most of the children in Liza's special world were the highly privileged offspring of Hollywood celebrities, only she had a veritable treasure trove of musical props and costumes. There were trunks loaded with canes, top hats, fake swords and daggers, tambourines, drums, magicians' tools, and other stage

30

accessories, dating from Judy's own vaudeville days. But even more magical were the hundreds of constantly replenished costumes that were carefully executed by Minnelli copying those of the big movies.

Sensing her advantage over the other children, Liza wisely decided not to share her bounty until she had proved her right to be the biggest star. Gayle Martin, Dean's daughter, taught her how to dance and, afterwards, Liza costumed herself and practised for hours in front of mirrors before inviting Gayle, Candice, and Mia Farrow to join her in creating 'live' versions of their favourite movie musicals. Soon most of Hollywood's moppet society was being enlisted for the staging of productions that were fully as lavish and nearly as professional as those created by Busby Berkeley, Edwin L. Marin, and Alfred E. Green for MGM's prolific series of 'gee, let's put on a show' celluloid musicals, many of which had teamed Mickey Rooney and Judy Garland.

Judy was a frequent observer of these miniature spectacles and, though she probably thought she was offering encouragement to the youngsters, her constant shouts to 'sing louder, kick higher' were usually construed as criticism, especially by the eager-to-please Liza. It was probably her mother's conviction, often expressed to the child, that Liza might some day become an acceptable dancer but never a competent singer that prompted the girl to idolise Fred Astaire and Cyd Charisse rather than any of MGM's array of singing stars.

Minnelli, though not so frequent an observer because of heavy film production schedules, viewed the home musicals in the context in which they were presented and he saw no need for criticism. One evening, he sat in full evening dress, utterly enchanted by the youngsters' efforts and oblivious to the fact that he had been planning to attend a dinner party.

In fact, Vincente was devoting more and more time to his daughter, who, he realised, was not experiencing the healthiest of childhoods. The blame, he felt, was as much his as Judy's. They were two emotionally and mentally wounded people unconsciously destroying each other because of past hurts and, ultimately, it would be little Liza who would suffer most. Living with one parent who was emotionally stable would be better for the child, he believed, than a continuation of the present overblown charade. Two incidents that occurred in the summer of 1950 reinforced the director's intention to encourage a final separation from Judy, though he felt himself incapable of making the actual irrevocable break.

The first came on June 20th and it made grotesquely clear the instabilities of both marital partners, the hopelessness of their future together, and the dangers their unhealthy relationship presented to Liza's well-being. Throughout the bizarre events of that traumatic evening, five-year-old Liza was alone and nearly forgotten—watching television and supposedly unaware of the melodramatic black comedy being played in full regalia all around her.

Judy had just been suspended by MGM for her failure to report to work in replacing the pregnant June Allyson in *Royal Wedding* (1951). Despondent but seemingly in control, she was at Minnelli's home pondering her future when she quietly excused herself and headed for the nearest bathroom. Several minutes later, Minnelli was startled by a piercing scream. Judy had slashed her neck with a broken water glass.

Insane with panic, a nearly hysterical Minnelli decided that this famous would-be suicide, his wife, just must not be found at his house but instead at what was now her legal residence on Sunset Boulevard. With the aid of neighbour Carleton Alsop, he called an ambulance for Judy's nearby Sunset Boulevard home and then discovered that a flock of anxious reporters were already assembled outside the Minnelli house, literally perched for the kill. Incredible as it seemed at the time, they already knew about the star's attempted suicide. It was later rumoured that Judy had herself called the press before making the rather feeble attempt on her life.

Somehow, Minnelli and Alsop managed to secrete a practically mummified Judy on the floor of Vincente's car and then sped to Judy's house where the ambulance was waiting. The doctor diagnosed the star's self-inflicted wounds as 'only a scratch', which was fortunate inasmuch as Minnelli's behaviour could have caused Judy's death had her injuries been more serious.

Even though she was no longer under contract to MGM, the studio had a proprietary interest in Judy because *Summer Stock* (1950), co-starring Gene Kelly and directed by Charles Walters, had not yet been released and Vincente was still very much under Metro contract. The circumstances surrounding the attempt on her life were withheld from the public. Indeed, it was generally believed (and reported) that she had slashed her wrists. Judy, who loved to joke about her repeated suicide attempts, never capitalised on the comic potential of *this* incident. It would remain a closely guarded secret for nearly a quarter of a century and then it would be Minnelli, himself, who would reveal the disturbing facts.

Judy and Minnelli did not separate immediately after her attempted suicide and, for a time, it appeared to Minnelli that they were closer than before.

The second and decisive incident that precipitated the final break-up of Judy and Vincente occurred in casual conversation when she admitted she had never told the truth to any of her psychiatrists—and there had been at least sixteen over the years. Minnelli was shocked. He felt that Judy had not tried to help herself, to cure herself of the demons that were plaguing her.

'So what?' she replied paranoiacally. 'There's more than one way to get even with you people.'

That ended it. Minnelli at last felt compelled to take the initiative. 'It was damn near impossible for me to forgive Judy for this. Liza's well-being would be better served if she had one stable parent living apart from his mate, rather than having two emotionally wounded parents living together,' he wrote in his autobiography.

Three days before Christmas of 1950, Judy kissed Liza goodbye and left for New York. Soon afterwards, she instituted divorce proceedings against Minnelli, charging mental cruelty and demanding custody of Liza. Minnelli did not contest, much to the surprise of those who knew of his devotion to Liza, but not of the circumstances surrounding Judy's suicide attempt.

The nightmare was over for Vincente.

For Liza, the real nightmare had barely begun.

CHAPTER FIVE

Liza remained with her father during Judy's sojourn in New York, and the early months of 1951 were probably among the happiest of the child's life. The mini-musicals of Liza and her friends continued at the Minnelli home, but without the critical interference from Judy that hitherto had somewhat inhibited the performers. At MGM, Liza was able to pursue her obsession for dancers and dancing on the set of Vincente's *An American in Paris* (1951), starring Gene Kelly and Leslie Caron, which was then in the final stages of production.

The idyll would soon end, for in New York, at a party given by Jackie Gleason, Judy had met Sid Luft, the man who was to shape the destinies of both mother and daughter. He was a promoter, a packager, and some believed, con man *extraordinaire*, and he arranged an engagement for Judy at the London Palladium. It was planned that Liza would attend, apparently at Vincente's insistence.

In his words, Minnelli explains that he believed Judy and Liza had been separated too long. 'Though I'd selfishly wanted Liza to myself,' he wrote in his autobiography, 'now was the time she should be with her mother—during one of Judy's greatest triumphs. Only then could Liza, who'd lived through so many of Judy's down periods, begin to understand her mother's staggering talent—and the personal cost by which it had been achieved.'

'Liza would also know,' wrote Minnelli, 'that, though her parents couldn't live together any longer, her father would always remain a Judy Garland fan.'

Minnelli took Liza to New York and placed his five-year-old daughter aboard a plane to London.

The Palladium debut, April 9th, 1951, was almost a disaster for Judy. During the opening number, which required some simple dance steps, the frightfully nervous Judy slipped and fell on her back, prematurely bringing the routine to a confused end. British audiences, traditionally less respectful towards performers than Americans, assumed the star was drunk and strongly voiced their disapproval.

The distraught Judy, stumbling frantically around the stage, suddenly heard Luft's voice shouting to her from a box, 'I love you. Sing! Sing!' She regained her composure, proved her sobriety, and went on with the show, scoring a personal triumph. There followed a sensationally successful tour throughout England, Wales, and Scotland. Judy had redeemed herself professionally.

Liza had witnessed her Mama at her show-stopping

best, and during the tour, she learned to address Luft as 'Uncle Sid'.

Judy's divorce from Minnelli was granted on March 3rd, 1952, and throughout this period Liza commuted between mother and father. When she was with Vincente, her life was serene. 'He really understood me,' Liza has said on repeated occasions. 'He treated me like such a lady. Even then, he dealt with me on a feminine level. To do that to a little girl is probably the most valuable thing that can happen.'

With Judy, life was anything but serene. Still, for a small child, it was enormously exciting and even sometimes frightening. One of Mama's most played 'games' with Liza was waking her in the middle of the night so that they could move to a new house or apartment. Sometimes they would slink out wearing layers of clothing, making their way stealthily into the night to avoid the marshals and sheriffs who were trying to confiscate Judy's belongings for non-payment of her escalating debts. In hotels, they would leave empty luggage as a 'joke' on the management. Liza was never directly told the real reason for the constant change of address, but she quickly caught on to its import. After all, it was not difficult for even a child to realise what was occurring when they were being locked out of hotel rooms by irate managements or when possessions were suddenly confiscated by official-looking men.

It was about this time, too, that Judy would sometimes become so emotionally unglued by the pills she was taking that she would feel herself an unfit mother, a junkie who should not be seen by children. At these times she would simply lock Liza out of their current lodgings. It might be for a few minutes, several hours, an entire day or, usually, until concerned neighbours intervened.

Shopkeepers in both Los Angeles and New York claim to have repeatedly provided snacks and sandwiches for a hungry, temporarily orphaned Liza. The suspicion exists, however, that on many occasions the child was merely acting out her hunger in order to beg free goodies. She was, after all, Judy's daughter and one of her first lessons in life was how to make an expert play for sympathy.

One evening, a few months after the divorce from Minnelli, Judy asked Liza if she would like it if Mama married 'Uncle Sid'.

'What for? Why would you want to do that?' responded the ever-practical Liza.

'Because,' replied Judy in what must have been her best stage voice, knowing even then that she was pregnant, 'if you do, my dear, then you could have a baby brother or sister.'

This made sense to Liza and she gave her tentative approval, probably imagining herself as flower girl or ring bearer at the ceremony.

She forgot about the conversation with her mother when she was again packed off to Minnelli in Hollywood while Judy played an engagement at the Curran Theatre in San Francisco. Then, on the evening of June 11th, 1952, Liza and Vincente were watching the news on TV when they learned that Judy and Luft had been married that day in San Francisco.

'I was shocked and I think Daddy was, too,' Liza recalled many years later, 'but I rationalised even then that it wasn't my business when Mama got married, really, or to whom.'

Minnelli would always remain 'Daddy' to Liza and she would reserve for him the special love that a child holds for her father. Luft would become 'Papa' or 'Papa Sid' and, even to Liza, he would always be something of an enigma.

Who was Sid Luft?

He had been born Michael Sidney Luft in New Rochelle, New York, in 1917, had attended the University of Pennsylvania, then later matriculated at the University of Miami. There were those who said he had been involved with aquacades in Ottowa, Canada, and that from 1940 to 1942 he was a member of the Royal Air Force. Other insiders recall that he had been a test pilot in the mid-1940s, and that he had drifted into agenting on the West Coast.

According to Jack L. Warner, the former long-reigning monarch of Warner Bros, Luft was '. . . one of the original guys who promised he'd never work a day in his life—and made good'. Warner, who claimed that Luft chiselled him out of thirty thousand dollars (and Jack was always known as a hard man to chisel, even for coffee money), sued, won judgment for the full amount and finally collected five hundred as full settlement.

'I'd kill him on the spot,' said Warner when confronted with the prospect of again meeting Luft, 'except for the fact that I wouldn't want to sit in the little green room at San Quentin.'

All Liza would really know about her new 'papa' was that he was rumoured to have underworld connections, that sometimes people took pot shots at him with rifles, and that he was formerly married to actress Lynn Bari, a long-reigning 'Queen of the Bs' at Twentieth Century-Fox studios, and that they had had a child. It would also become apparent that he did not take the roles of husband or father seriously and, ultimately, Liza would act as mother, father, sister, and benefactor for the Garland–Luft offspring, Lorna and Joey.

Once Liza had the audacity to ask exactly what Luft did in life. 'I'm in the suit business,' he is said to have replied. 'I sue people.'

Predictably, Judy's new marriage was not fated to last. Writing in *McCall's* magazine in 1964, she stated, 'The birth of our daughter, Lorna, was the only bright spot in the first year of our marriage. From the beginning, Sid and I weren't happy. I don't know why. I really don't.'

The Lufts settled in Hollywood, at fashionable Holmby Hills, and Liza was again able to be with her father often. Minnelli was completing *The Band Wagon* (1953) at MGM with Liza's favourite stars, Fred Astaire and Cyd Charisse, so Liza was an almost constant visitor to the set.

After Lorna was born on November 21st, 1952, Judy went to work at Warner Bros in *A Star Is Born* (1954). Her record-breaking nineteen-week engagement at the famed Palace Theatre in New York the previous winter had made her a hot box-office name again, and Jack L. Warner envisioned Judy's comeback vehicle as a blockbuster to surpass all blockbusters. He had Humphrey Bogart contracted to co-star with Judy, a combination that guaranteed box-office dynamite, but Luft, who had hoped for Cary Grant for the role, insisted that James Mason play the part instead—and, probably because Mason worked more cheaply than Bogart, it was Luft's will that prevailed.

Liza was not much interested in *A Star Is Born*. She could always see and hear Mama at home and, besides, the domestic life at the Lufts had become stormy to a point where neighbours were complaining about the sights and sounds of battle between Judy and Sid. For Liza, life at home was becoming extremely uncomfortable.

She had, over the years, developed what she calls 'a real horror of angry, screaming voices' and this, all too often, seemed to be the only manner of communication between the embattled Lufts. To be sure, Sid was often away on his mysterious business trips and when this happened it often placed awesome responsibilities on a seven-year-old child.

With her new papa, Liza had inherited Luft's son, Johnny, eighteen months younger than Liza, and then the infant Lorna. Since nurses and servants often could not cope with Judy's sudden and severe temper tantrums, it was sometimes left to little Liza to act as the children's mother. She recalls one particularly dramatic night when Judy stormed out of the house after arguing violently with Lorna's nurse. The irate nurse then departed, leaving Liza alone with a wailing baby. She did not know how to change nappies or to provide the infant with its bottle and she could not imagine when her impulsive mother might return, if ever. Judy did come back, of course, though it was many hours later, and the next day precocious Liza demanded that she be taught the care and feeding of young children.

Liza showered tremendous love on baby Lorna and, later, on Lorna's younger brother, Joey, as if by proving her devotion to them she could earn their love in return. Though she has never explicitly said so publicly, chances are that Liza continually felt like an outsider in the Luft menagerie. She was certain of Vincente's love and she saw him often, but Liza also knew that she was no longer 'his' in the eyes of the courts and she probably was sensitive enough to feel like a poor relative among the Lufts, the 'other' child who sometimes lives with the family.

The evidence seems ample that Liza had indeed become the outsider in Judy's life. When she was sent to a country camp a short distance from Los Angeles for several months, Minnelli visited the obviously lonesome and unhappy Liza every weekend. Judy, the camp counsellor recorded, came only twice for brief reunions with her daughter.

Actually, Judy often seemed to regard her first-born as something akin to an early misfortune above which one somehow rises. Her other children were brighter and more talented, she believed, until Liza began making a real show business name for herself—and even then Judy contended that, although Liza might skyrocket to stardom, Lorna, if she so chose, would find a slower, steadier, and more lasting fame.

Judy always carried two photographs in her purse. One was 'family' and the other a picture taken at the Beverly Hilton Hotel showing Judy with President John F. Kennedy. The family photo lovingly posed Judy with Lorna and Joey, but not Liza, although there were many less cherished shots that did include the elder daughter. Despite every indication to the contrary, Judy also liked to boast that she would not make the same mistakes with Lorna and Joey that she had made with Liza.

Perhaps the star's attitude towards her daughter was most clearly expressed when Liza, then aged twenty, played a summer stock engagement against her mother's clearly expressed orders. 'You are an admirable young woman,' Judy wrote her, 'but you exasperate me.'

Equally revealing is Lorna's recollection that Liza simply was not a part of her early life. She admits to having deliberately blocked out the unhappy memories of childhood. Even so, it seems strange that Liza did not seem to exist to her half-sister until Lorna was twelve and nineteen-year-old Liza had already achieved her own prominence in show business.

Liza has no such memory blocks. She claims to remember *everything* in extraordinarily vivid, precise detail. The trouble is that she is inclined towards overstatement or understatement, and outrageous fantasising, sometimes all within the span of a single sentence. She calls the undoubtedly self-protective fabrications 'memory trips' in which she invents the stories she believes people most want to hear. Yet Liza also professes an obligation to tell the truth concerning her mother because she '. . . let the legend go so far . . . she let it get so far out of hand'. There are those close to Liza, however, who believe that by now she has spun so many fantasies concerning herself and her strange past that she is emotionally incapable

43

of relating the truth about anything over a sustained period of time.

Liza seems to acknowledge this possibility self-defensively. 'People always think they're honest,' she has said. 'But they're not really. They are their own dreams of what they would like to be.'

In a conscious effort to preserve the dreams and illusions she has structured on the past, Liza has steadfastly resisted professional analysis. She prefers to 'waft'.

'Wafting,' she explains to the uninitiated, 'is when you pretend that you're not really you. You're like a cork bobbing on the ocean. No matter how rough the water is, the cork stays afloat. Nothing can stop it.'

'I'm not putting psychiatry down,' she has stressed, 'but there are doors I don't want opened, not just yet. If I go to a shrink, he might tell me some things I hadn't thought about myself and I might not like them—and I might not wake up the next morning.'

Though she chooses not to recognise the emotional scars, the past has left its psychological mark. Like her mother, she bites her nails to the point where the nubs sometimes bleed. Like Judy, Liza the woman cannot bear to be alone—and, fortunately, she is now in a position where she seldom has to be. She feels compelled to show affection and to give love, especially to those she fears might otherwise be unloved. Most often, she needs to be reassured that she really is loved. Scenes of unpleasantness, particularly of anger, are avoided at all costs. Her eyes will glaze, her mind will wander, and she will somehow spiritually remove herself from the troublesome situation. If she senses prolonged difficulties, Liza simply packs her belongings and moves away, so as to be, in her own words, 'a moving target'. Ever an enigma, she tries to use toughness and a battery of show-bizzy poses and assaults to hide her vulnerability and she exploits her vulnerability to disguise her underlying toughness.

The real horrors that Liza faced in childhood will probably remain sheltered in her mind, having already been replaced in the public record by the sometimes oddly comic fabrications and other times nightmare-like fictions that enable the public both to envy effervescent Liza for the exciting life drama that has been hers and, simultaneously, to sympathise with her in her traumas. In the course of her complex, hectic life, she has created so many fictions concerning herself that she has become, in effect, the sum product of those fictions. The real Liza, the woman scarred and wounded by the fixating traumas of childhood, may now be so deeply buried within the subconscious that she may never emerge to challenge the identity of the role Liza has chosen to play.

'Reality,' in Liza's rule book, remains 'something you rise above'.

There is little reality in many of the distorted stories Liza tells, usually in a bid to gain sympathy. The sixteen or twenty-two schools she alternately claims to have attended in her gypsy-style childhood actually numbered about eight, while the fourteen times she insisted she auditioned for the Broadway production of *Cabaret* can be reduced, in point of fact, to one hearing granted as no more than a courtesy because the producers and librettists of the show were insistent on having a British girl in the lead.

Among Liza's zanier and presumably more fanciful

45

'memories' of childhood is the one in which, at age eleven, she was hiring the complement of household servants, demanding references and passing judgments on their capabilities and suitability for continued employment. This fiction seems almost as apocryphal as the tale that she regularly drove Lorna and Joey to school when she was thirteen because the family chauffeur was always drunk.

A very real event, however, was Judy's appearance at the Palace Theatre in 1956. Though not as successful as the earlier engagement in 1951, it did afford Liza the opportunity to appear on stage with her mother one Saturday evening near the end of the run. Rock Hudson lifted the girl up on to the stage and while Judy sang *Swanee*, Liza danced. All the time the child was wondering if her panties were showing. Afterwards, the theatre manager gave the child a five-dollar bill as payment for her special performance. Even this modest incident would later be revised in the interest of family solidarity, with Liza claiming that Luft had given her the money.

Real, too, were Judy's repeated suicide attempts and Liza's recurrent efforts to thwart, circumvent, or humour them. What actually went on nobody knows or is willing, at this point, to reveal. Liza claims that she and Lorna, the children then being about twelve and five respectively, used to empty the contents of Mama's capsules and refill them with sugar so that when Judy overdosed herself the consequences would be no more severe than an upset stomach due to an excess of glucose in her system. At other times, Judy's threats of imminent self-destruction were simply pathetic bids for attention, with the star consuming a few aspirins and then childishly holding her breath to assume a posture of death.

Liza was later to claim that saving her mother from death became one of her essential household duties, like washing the dishes or sweeping the floor, mundane tasks with which the privileged child probably only concerned herself in her Dickensian fantasies as the family chimney sweep. It is known, however, that a teenaged Liza did order a stomach pump as a precautionary measure in case traumatised Judy actually did overdose herself.

Far more disrupting, probably, to young and sensitively impressionable minds were Judy's increasingly frequent periods of pill and liquor-induced irrationality. These would be the times when she would be apt to lock the children out of the house (or hotel suite) and leave them, literally, to scavenge for themselves.

Even these incidents would serve Liza's fertile imagination. In *Time* magazine in 1970, she is quoted as saying that she was sixteen when Judy precipitated her actual break from home and family. 'Mama went on a kick every now and then where she used to kick me out of the house. Usually, I'd stand outside the door, and pretty soon she'd open it and we'd fall into each other's arms, crying and carrying on. But one day she did it and I took her up on it. I had my plane fare and a hundred dollars, and I've never taken a penny since.'

And that, supposedly, is how fifteen-and-a-half-year-old Liza started her professional career! It is a telling scene that the adolescent probably would have dearly loved to play, and undoubtedly did many times in her 'memory trips'. But it is as unreal as the image Liza presents of herself as the teenage household drudge who just happened to have a transcontinental plane fare and one hundred dollars hidden in her bobby-sox.

The way Judy remembers the real start of Liza's professional career, and the way Vincente Minnelli confirms it, Liza was in Paris, studying at the Sorbonne, when she decided that she wanted a career as an entertainer. The child sent a telegram to Judy in Las Vegas, where the superstar was fulfilling a casino play date. It read, 'Dear Mama: I'm coming home. I want to talk to you. Love, Liza.'

'I knew what it was immediately,' Judy later recalled. 'I think she decided to go into show business when she was an embryo, she kicked so much.'

'When the wire arrived,' Judy reflected in a *Look* magazine interview, 'all I could think about was this child flying half the way around the world, all the time rehearsing what she would say.

'Then I started rehearsing what I would say,' Judy continued: 'all sorts of motherly things about going back to school. Liza was off the plane practically before the door was opened. She charged right up to me. I shot the works. "Liza, darling," I said, "why don't you go into show business?" Then we both started crying right there at the airport and it got very messy and happy.'

As Judy implied, Liza's serious decision to seek a performing career was never the shock and disappointment to her family that Liza has widely maintained for so many years. From the start the child was bred, like a racehorse, for stardom. She was a thoroughbred and she was never long out of the spot-light.

In 1954, she made an unbilled appearance with Lucille Ball and Desi Arnaz in Minnelli's *The Long, Long Trailer* at MGM. Although the bit was cut from release prints, her 'contribution' to the wedding party sequence was widely publicised at the time.

The year 1955 saw her interviewed on nationwide television by family friend Art Linkletter, who bluntly asked her whether she hoped Judy's current pregnancy would bring her a sister or a brother. 'A girl,' the young Liza promptly replied, adding with a show-bizzy (and probably pre-rehearsed) show of disgust, 'boys are too messy.'

Liza, however, learned to adjust when Joseph Wiley Luft was born, March 29th, 1955, the day before the Academy Award ceremonies in which Judy, nominated as Best Actress of the Year for *A Star Is Born*, would lose to socialite Grace Kelly (*The Country Girl*) in what Groucho Marx would characterise as '. . . the greatest robbery since Brinks'.

Liza's next major public appearance would come in December of 1956 when she made an awkward showing on television co-hosting with Bert Lahr the first network telecast of Judy's classic feature, *The Wizard of Oz* (1939).

Nearly two years passed before Liza made her next national appearance, unrewardingly, on *The Jack Paar Show*. The public saw her again in April, 1959, when she sang and danced with convivial Gene Kelly to the tune of *For Me and My Gal* on his TV special. Nobody, then, seemed much impressed by her talents and her next comeback, again ignored by the public at large, was in singing *Over the Rainbow* on *The Hedda Hopper Showcase* in January, 1960. At this time, Liza weighed a more than flabby 11 stones 11 pounds.

It was next decided to provide Liza with professional training at the famed High School of the Performing Arts in New York City. It was here that she had her first recorded romance, the recipient of her feelings being fellow student Bobby Mariano, who worked after classes in the chorus of the Dick Van Dyke–Chita Rivera musical, *Bye, Bye Birdie*. Liza literally became a 'stage door Jane', mooning over Bobby and dreaming of the time when she would become a Broadway gypsy, dancing in the chorus of a big-time show. The closest she was to come, then, to her goal was a Veterans' Hospital benefit in Harlem where she and other students performed the 'Steam Heat' number from *Pajama Game*.

Liza was convinced she was deeply in love with Bobby, but another student, Marvin Hamlisch, was her best friend and the first of the undiscovered talents that she would enlist in professional association. (It was with Marvin that she made an amateurish demonstration record in an effort to interest producers and disc companies in her singing talents. No one was impressed.) Hamlisch was an unknown when he began composing vocal arrangements and providing musical co-ordination for Liza's nightclub act and recording sessions. His public obscurity ended, in 1974, when he received Academy Awards for the title song in *The Way We Were* and for the even more popular arrangements of old Scott Joplin ragtime tunes for *The Sting*.

The competition at the School of the Performing Arts may have proved a bit stiff for the hardly unknown but still professionally unblossomed Liza since, in the late spring of 1961, she was enrolled in the public high school at Scarsdale, New York, a fashionable suburb of New York City, known more for its predilections for Beefeater, Tanqueray, and Chivas Regal than things theatrical.

To prepare her for the challenge of the drama club at Scarsdale High, it was decided that Liza would spend the summer months apprenticing (for free) at the Cape Cod Melody Tent in Hyannis, Massachusetts. Selecting that particular music tent for Liza's tutelage period was not just chance. Like others hovering around the glow of President John F. Kennedy's summer White House at Hyannisport, Judy had decided to vacation nearby. Among the other 'humble' apprentices at the 1,500-seat theatre-in-the-round was Cressida Gaitskell, daughter of Hugh Gaitskell, then head of the British Labour Party. (On one occasion that season, Cressida was invited to dine with the Presidential party on the Presidential yacht.) But Liza had one status symbol that was impressive to even the loftiest of her co-workers–she had an agent.

The music tent was controlled by Manhattan theatrical attorney David Holtzmann, who supervised the seasonal operations, aided by members of his family and other hired assistants. Liza appeared, without visible distinction, in the choruses of *Wish You Were Here*, *Flower Drum Song*, and other standard straw hat fare. However, for the week's run of *Take Me Along*, based on Eugene O'Neill's *Ah, Wilderness*, Liza was elevated into a role of semi-importance as Muriel Macomber, the ingenue who sings the song *I Would Die*.

Much publicity was made over the fact that Judy would actually be among the opening night's audience, but repeated, frantic checks of the crowd-in-the-round revealed no effervescent Miss Garland. No one, apparently, was more disappointed than Liza, who wanted to show Mama just how much entertainment savvy she had acquired at the Tent. Judy later explained that she had not wanted to steal Liza's thunder on that important evening, and made amends by coming to a performance later in the week, and then joining her daughter and other cast members backstage for an impromptu party. Liza, dressed in her persistent offstage garb of black leotards, puffing on cigarettes more for effect than pleasure, and chewing vociferously on gum, was coming of age.

That September, Liza was living in Scarsdale with one of her papa's relatives. (Judy would flit in and out of the vicinity, for she was dating André Philippe at that time, an aspiring performer who resided in the area.)

It came as no surprise to Liza's fellow students at Scarsdale High when the summer stock 'veteran' was cast in the leading role of the drama club's production of *The Diary of Anne Frank*. Liza, at long last, scored the personal triumph for which she had been so thoroughly prepared. And it was not allowed to go unnoticed.

Still, the Scarsdale experience was not a happy one for young Liza. The students understandably resented her professional clout and she, perhaps ingenuously unaware of how much power was secretly exerted behind the scenes, resented the snobbishness, insularity, and provincialism of the community. She felt that Scarsdale's only sophistication and self-interest lay in its own boring standards of dress, deportment, and discretion—each an area in which the maturing Liza was sorely deficient at the time. Her long, unstyled hair, someone said, was like a forest of evil, and her clothes, by Scarsdale's fashion-plate standards, were simply a mess.

'Clothes weren't as interesting then as they are now,' explains the girl who in recent years has been named one of the world's best dressed women. 'I was neat, but a zipper would always be unzipped on my pleated skirt and my hair wouldn't always be perfectly combed.'

Liza made another mistake with her classmates by trying to impress them with tales about her friendship with such stars as Marilyn Monroe who, she claimed, always sought her out at parties. Liza also talked too much about her 'adult' relationship with movie idol George Hamilton upon whom she had developed a teenie-bopper crush when she visited her father on location for the Texas-set *Home from the Hill*, starring Robert Mitchum, Eleanor Parker, George Peppard, and Hamilton.

It did not work. Nobody seemed to believe the stories and as for the glamour she tried to generate through her family and personal associations, the other kids soon began to regard the plump, sloppy, and gum-chewing Liza as strictly a trog.

Next, Liza self-defensively adopted the attitude of *noblesse oblige* that even now typifies her attitude towards her Scarsdale schoolmates.

'I couldn't find anybody that was as bright as I

was,' she later carped. 'I guess it was because I grew up with adults . . . kids just weren't into adult conversation, like philosophy or literature or anything like that. I'd start a conversation and nobody would join in.'

Chances are, however, that Liza's efforts at conversation were a great deal less sophisticated than she imagined. Art Linkletter, a neighbour of the Lufts, had some less than enthusiastic remarks about the conversational quality in the Garland household in his recent book, *Women Are My Favourite People*.

'The talk at her [Judy's] parties,' Linkletter wrote, 'reminded me of the old gag about the actor who, after boring everyone for an eternity with his latest exploits, finally turns to a companion and says: "Well, enough about me! Let's talk about you. What did you think of my last movie?" '

Life in Scarsdale, particularly now that Judy had departed the environs, became so unendurable for the lonely Liza that she determined to test her abilities as an actress in a real-life situation. Feeling she had to get away from Snob Town, USA, she concocted a story for school authorities about a family crisis that demanded her presence in London.

'I acted—God, how I acted,' Liza later recalled.

The ruse worked. She charged a ticket with a travel agency that she knew was fully accustomed to the family's peculiar transient ways and she flew immediately to London, where she wandered about Piccadilly and Soho before contacting a friend upon whom she unleashed her heartbreak. According to those close to Liza, the friend happened to be the flower seller at Charing Cross Station. Emotionally catharsised, Liza then made the return to New York and to Scarsdale, all within the space of a single day!

Only after her *Anne Frank* triumph at Scarsdale High did Liza make friends in Scarsdale and she chose them with a flair for the dramatic. Her constant companions were twin girls, WASP blondes, who strikingly served as living bookends wherever the wide-eyed, swarthily complexioned outsider appeared. One of Liza's Scarsdale classmates, enchanted neither by the Liza of 1961 nor of today, recalls those times: 'My God, what a sight it was,' he said. 'It was as though she had a personal Mafia guarding her. She was a girl with power—and she knew that we were on to her. That's why she hated Scarsdale and that's why Scarsdale couldn't stand her.'

Another classmate, Ethel Geisinger, remembers it differently. Ethel had been in Scarsdale only a year when Liza arrived and, like Liza, she had found the students insular, self-centred, and snobbishly indifferent to all outsiders. Their friends were children they had grown up with since infancy, and they did not want to make new ones unless they happened to be capable of bringing the community and school new status and prestige.

'I had a difficult time in Scarsdale,' Ethel Geisinger recalls, 'but for Liza it must have been much harder.

'There was so much excitement at the school when we learned that Judy Garland's daughter had enrolled that nobody could have lived up to the expectation. Then this plump, plain-looking girl arrived. I guess she tried at first to fit in, but this was impossible, and then she just withdrew into herself. Liza was always pleasant and nice, yet she never really seemed to be there. It was like she had decided to be a loner and if she ever decided to have friends she would select them. Finally, after she did *Anne Frank* with the drama club, she picked the twins. They were nice girls, outsiders like herself.'

Ethel disputes the tales about Liza's reputed messiness.

'It's just not true that she was terribly dirty and sloppy. I mean she did bathe and her clothes were always clean and well pressed, but just sort of thrown together on her body as if she didn't care how she looked. She was drab, maybe consciously so, and I remember one day the kids were laughing at her because her bobby-sox didn't match. Things like that were terribly important in Scarsdale.

'I remember, too, some final examination, either maths or science, and Liza got this really terrible grade—like 27 or something—and everybody felt so superior to Judy Garland's dumb-dumb daughter.

'She was good in *Anne Frank* though, really good, and the next year after she had left school and opened off-Broadway in *Best Foot Forward*, all the kids went to see her in the show and you would have thought she had been the most popular girl in school.'

Liza earned a reprieve from Scarsdale in early 1962 when she went to Los Angeles with her mother for the filming of John Cassavetes' *A Child Is Waiting*, co-starring Judy's close friend, Burt Lancaster. It was a strong, though commercially unsuccessful drama about mental retardation and Liza spent day after day showering affection and attention upon the retarded youngsters who appeared in the black-and-white film.

By March, she was back in Scarsdale and again unhappy until it was learned that Mama would be going to London in May to film *The Lonely Stage*, a film that would be released in America as *I Could Go On Singing*. Liza and her *Anne Frank* co-players were scheduled to go to Europe that summer (Judy had 'anonymously' donated funds for the high schoolers to perform their production in a vacation tour through Italy, Greece, the Netherlands, and Israel). At first, it was felt that Liza should remain in Scarsdale for the remainder of the school term. However, the tenacious adolescent's will prevailed, and she journeyed to London with Mama, Lorna, and Joey.

Sometime during 1962, Liza, to her later embarrassment recorded the voice of Dorothy for a feature-length cartoon film that has alternately been called *Return to Oz* and sometimes *Journey Back to Oz*. The film, which also used the voices of Milton Berle, Mickey Rooney, Herschel Bernardi, Ethel Merman, and Margaret Hamilton (of the original MGM version) was an overt capitalisation of the Garland image and of the earlier classic picture, and all Liza was required to do was sing a few songs and mimic Judy's voice for the sound track.

None the less, Mama went all out to promote Liza's cartoon film. It proved a futile, if well-intended gesture. There had been a rash of unsuccessful cartoon features with well-known voices, including Judy's own *Gay Purr-ee* (1963), and the new *Oz* movie would remain virtually unseen until the early 1970s when it had an ignominious world première in Australia. It would receive some strange publicity from Filmation Associates preparatory to its American release:

What is LIZA MINNELLI doing to HERSCEL BERNARDI?
What is ETHEL MERMAN doing to MICKEY ROONEY?
What is HERSCHEL BERNARDI doing to LIZA MINNELLI?
What is SAMMY CAHN doing to JIMMY VAN HEUSEN?
What is JACK E. LEONARD doing to LIZA MINNELLI?
What is PAUL LYNDE doing to MARGARET HAMILTON?
What is DANNY THOMAS doing to MILTON BERLE? . . .
You'll find out when you see this year's most
exciting fun-filled animated musical motion picture. . .

When *Journey Back to Oz* was pushed into minor British release in early 1973, one British trade paper would report of the eighty-eight minute rip-off, '. . . all is not well in Oz . . . the action of the film is rather unimaginative and repetitive.' The English reviewer did have a kind word for Liza's soundtrack performance: '. . . [her] quiet, intelligent reading of Dorothy strikes just the right note. . . .'

After receiving the equivalent of a high school diploma in London and making the *Anne Frank* continental trek with her one-time classmates, wide-eyed Liza was sent to Paris in the fall of 1962 to study at the Sorbonne. Liza loved Paris, but she was restless and she knew now that her future, her whole life, lay in show business.

'I knew what I wanted to do and I had it out with myself,' Liza soon thereafter told a *Saturday Evening Post* interviewer. 'I wanted to live in New York on my own and take lessons in singing and dancing and acting and see if I could do anything.'

licity pose for the NBC-TV Special *Liza* (June, 1970).

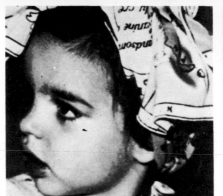

The young Liza.

On the set of MGM's
Summer Stock (1950)
with Mama.

Rehearsing with Gene Kelly for his April,
1959, CBS-TV Special.

With Lorna, Judy, Sid Luft, and Joey in
their Hollywood home in 1962.

With Lorna Luft at CBS-TV, viewing
The Wizard of Oz in 1956.

(*above*) With Albert Finney in *Charlie Bubbles* (Regional, 1968).

(*below*) With Peter Allen (c. 1969).

On CBS-TV's 'The Judy Garland Show' in November, 1963.

The *Buckle Down Winsocki* finale number from *Best Foot Forward* (1963).

In *The Sterile Cuckoo* (Paramount, 1969).

With Wendell Burton in *The Sterile Cuckoo*.

With Wendell Burton in *The Sterile Cuckoo*.

Pookie Adams' finale in *The Sterile Cuckoo*.

With Barbara Logan in *Tell Me That You Love Me, Junie Moon* (Paramount, 1970).

As the Kit Kat Klub star of *Cabaret*.

With Joel Grey in the *Money, Money, Money* number from *Cabaret*.

As Sally Bowles in *Cabaret* (ABC Pictures—Allied Artists, 1972).

With Michael York in *Cabaret*.

With Marisa Berenson in *Cabaret*.

With Fred Ebb and Bob Fosse in 1972.

With Lucille Ball and Goldie Hawn in Las Vegas (Autumn, 1972).

The *Ring Them Bells* number from the CBS-TV Special *Liza with a Z.*

Preparing for the Royal Command Performance at the London Palladium in May, 1972, with Dan Rowan and Dick Martin.

CHAPTER SIX

After Liza's initial, rather encouraging meeting with Mama in Las Vegas, she discovered that Judy's blessings on her potential show business career could be a double-edged affair. Judy, who one minute could be warm, generous, and understanding, and the next be the opposite, informed Liza a few days later, 'Okay, if that's what you really want to do, go ahead. Just one thing, no more money from me again—ever again. You're on your own, baby.'

Liza was then sixteen years old.

Granted there was an element in Judy's 'threat' which smacked of jealousy against her own daughter, who might one day usurp Garland's spotlight. However, Judy's attitude on the whole was neither as heartless nor as unwise as it might first appear. She did agree to continue supplying Liza with clothing and 'incidentals', these including musical arrangements, acting class tuitions, and emergency funds. All Liza really was expected to do was to provide herself with the daily needs of independent living. Besides, Judy fully knew, Minnelli would always be quick to offer a generous helping hand whether needed or not.

Also, it should be remembered that Garland had been enduring one of her most difficult career periods. She had recently had one of her greatest public triumphs, at Carnegie Hall on April 23rd, 1961, but she also recognised it as a curious defeat, the end of 'the girl next door' and the beginning of Judy Garland as a cult figure. She could no longer belong to the masses and for ever more would be a camp figure. It was an image she accepted because she had no other choice, but she did not really wish it for herself and certainly not for her oldest child.

'When I die, my darling,' she told Liza, 'they'll fly the flag at half mast on Fire Island. I can see them now, standing at the meat rack, singing "Somewhere over the . . .".' (Indeed that wooden area in Cherry Grove, renowned as *the* most active spot of homosexual fun and games on the East Coast, is now affectionately called by the natives, 'The Judy Garland Memorial Park'.)

Judy did not want such camp adulation/denigration for Liza. She would not let that happen to Liza. She would force Liza to be super tough as she had never been tough herself. Judy realised she had not been the good mother she had wanted to be but she also understood that her new role as the wicked witch could be a beneficial one. If that's what would help ensure her daughter's future, she would play the role of lady monster to the hilt. Judy knew, too, that she was moving into some ugly times ahead, periods that could damage and hurt Liza and which, in all likelihood could destroy her own life. If Judy in this transitional period was suicidal, it was merely the natural impulse of someone who had nearly reached the end of a mangled rope.

Garland's marriage to Luft was at an end after innumerable separations and this time the severance would be brutal beyond belief. Sid demanded custody of Lorna and Joey and he was willing, even anxious it seemed, to expose Judy Garland for the monster that he repeatedly claimed lay beyond the public figure.

Liza, if really on her own, could at least be spared the full brunt of the engulfing ugliness that was approaching.

Luft was to charge that his wife was 'an emotionally disturbed and unbalanced person' who had attempted suicide more than twenty times. In an affidavit, Luft stated, 'On at least three occasions during 1963 and on numerous previous occasions she had taken overdoses of barbiturates. On six occasions she has attempted suicide by slashing herself on her wrists, elbows or throat.' And this was only the beginning of the ugly so-called 'truth'.

Luft would provide witnesses, former household servants, who would testify to Judy's alcoholism which, after bouts of hepatitis and liver disease, consisted exclusively of consuming each day two to four bottles of Liebfraumilch, a light German wine. Judy sometimes became so drunk, the clinical statements continued, that she abused the children in a loud, intoxicated manner and once she was alleged to have exhibited herself naked before hotel employees.

Judy, in turn, charged that Luft had beaten her with his fists and several times had attempted to strangle her. Finally, she had become so frightened that she had hired bodyguards and detectives to protect herself and the children. This inspired Luft to assert that Judy's 'thugs' had beaten him up and, when Judy's entourage (detectives included) departed for London, he pressed kidnapping charges against her.

The situation was not resolved until November of 1965 when Judy was awarded her long-sought divorce and won custody of the children. By that time, Liza, with much secret assistance from her mother, was well on the road to stardom.

Liza Minnelli, at age sixteen, was 5′ 4½″ and weighed approximately ten stones. Like Judy, she was still a compulsive nail biter and she had an unending flow of nervous energy that could be both a turn-on and a turn-off.

When she arrived in New York, all she had was one hundred dollars in savings, the framed five dollars the manager of the Palace had bestowed on her, and a temporary home with family friends.

She found a brief job modelling teenage fashions for *Seventeen* magazine and took as much time as possible to study acting at the Herbert Berghof studio in Greenwich Village, and later she would take voice lessons with David Soren Collyer, the West 67th Street speech therapist who had coached Judy at one point in her career. In February, 1963, she participated in recitations of Robert Frost's poetry. Judy, who usually managed to avoid Liza's public openings, was present and, in a word, devastated. There was a naturalness and truth in Liza's delivery, a childlike freedom that was both disturbing in its vulnerability and striking in its raw power. Judy, now more than ever, was fearful that without strong discipline Liza would somehow misuse her talent and fall into a pattern like her own.

But she had made Liza independent and the girl had gone bohemian in freakish New York, impressed by the Beatnik way of life. Judy had deliberately abrogated her maternal authority and now she was guilt-ridden, convinced that she had made a disastrous mistake.

Almost immediately thereafter, however, Liza had exciting news of her own. She had an opportunity to audition for a major role in a revival of *Best Foot Forward*, the 1941 Broadway musical with a score by Hugh Martin and Ralph Blane.

'Mama was so great when I told her,' Liza said soon after. 'I called her in California and you should have heard her. She got so nervous and she started telling me to relax and remember my poise and not get nervous and what was I going to sing and should she fly out special arrangements. . . . Wow, she was funny. She was a nervous wreck.'

Liza could not have known then that the show's producers, anxious to make a financial return in the precarious theatrical scene of the 1960s, were intent on casting the child of a famous star in order to give the decidedly seedy revival some box-office lustre. And the threadbare show would need something, for it was to be housed in the annexe of a very permissive bar. No one would be better suited for the audience-grabbing gimmick than Judy Garland's daughter, talented or not.

A frightened, shaking Liza arrived for the audition twenty minutes late, certain she had already blown her opportunity. She warbled two songs, *The Way You Look Tonight* and *They Can't Take that Away from Me*. Producer Arthur Whitelaw was sufficiently impressed by the girl's genuine talent to have her role enlarged and a new song, *You Are for Loving*, especially written for her.

Eagerly, Liza plunged into rehearsal determined to prove herself and, instead, broke her foot during the first dance rehearsal. The opening of the show was postponed and Liza spent her seventeenth birthday, dejectedly, in a hospital.

Judy, meanwhile, had secretly arranged an appearance for Liza on television's *The Jack Paar Show*. She knew that Paar, a close friend, would allow Liza an effective showcase and that he would enable her to display her natural warmth. She even tried to make Liza believe that her broken foot would prove a great advantage on television. 'Make sure they see your cast,' Judy advised, and she also urged that Liza look visibly pained on occasion in the best 'show must go on' tradition.

The Paar appearance was a minor triumph. Introduced to the television audience as Dyju Langard, a new Armenian discovery, the crippled girl sang in native Americanese and earned a strong ovation before her real identity was pixie-ishly revealed by Paar.

By the time *Best Foot Forward* finally opened on April 2nd, 1963, at the Stage 73 Theatre, it had achieved an aura of importance unprecedented for off-Broadway theatre. It was all due to the presence in the cast of Judy Garland's daughter, and press representatives Max Eisen and Rex Reed, the latter not yet graduated from the shadows of anonymity, did everything possible to play up this gimmick.

Police barricades were erected to cope with the opening-night crowds which might not have seemed so huge had the theatre housing 'New York's first off-Hollywood show' seated more than 187 persons. The capacity of the unlush house did create a limit on the numbers who could attend the opening so, except for the critics, it was a strictly 'A' group crowd.

There was, however, an empty seat in the second row, the place that had been reserved for Judy Garland. Some said that she was secluded at the Plaza Hotel, drunk out of her mind, while others, more loyal to Judy, insisted that she was simply too frightened on Liza's behalf to attend such an occasion.

In the interval, Liza frantically telephoned the hotel and awakened a sleeping Judy who, in turn, hysterically maintained that the opening was supposed to be *tomorrow* night. None the less, at the post-theatre party at Sardi's, Liza found a note and a bottle of champagne from Judy. Later, Liza would claim that Judy deliberately did not attend the opening so as not to attract attention away from the show.

Judy did attend the second night, with a battalion of photographers in tow. As she stated at the time, 'I cried and cried. I was so proud of my baby. She had worked so hard and done it all alone. And you know Liza's the first one of us to do this. I never had a Broadway show.' Judy never did get around to voicing her thoughts about the quality of Liza's performance and neither, for the most part, did the gentlemanly critics of the day.

On opening night, Liza's foot was still in a cast and she was unable to perform the dance numbers. It was a strange situation, since she was the show's major dancer. Thus the reviewers had to content themselves with judging a presence rather than a full-bodied performance. Also, few wished to be really churlish in hastily dismissing an adolescent cripple who had not really had the opportunity to exhibit her talent.

Walter Kerr, then the dean of the New York drama critics, set the tone which the others were to follow in assessing Liza's stage debut. 'Liza Minnelli', Kerr penned, 'is certainly appealing, and would be even if she wasn't Judy Garland's daughter.'

Faint praise, but praise none the less, and the trend-conscious *Theatre World* yearbook was quick to bestow upon Liza a 'Promising Personality Award'. She was one of twelve such newcomers lauded that year by Daniel Blum.

In point of fact, Liza's performance in *Best Foot Forward* was not very substantial. She had been cast in the rowdy soubrette role of Ethel Hofflinger, created by Nancy Walker in the original production. It called for toughness . . . and Liza merely offered vulnerability. She literally stumbled through most of the role, shining in occasional musical moments but seemingly unable to relate to her particular role or to other members of the cast. The characterisation would have been vaguely embarrassing had not Liza had the 'eleven o'clock song', her only solo, *You Are for Loving*. Unencumbered by the stale dialogue of the John Cecil Holm book or the demand for role-playing, she transformed a banal ballad into the only genuinely effective moment of the show. For the first time, the general public could witness Liza's enormous potential.

Liza's 45 rpm recording of *You Are for Loving*, recorded separately from the version in the cast LP album, sold nearly a half-million copies and suddenly she was in demand for TV appearances. Between March and June, she lost more than twenty pounds and made an awkward appearance on *The Ed Sullivan Show*. 'The most promising actress of the year really was terrible,' Liza later recalled. 'I was scared knock-kneed and it showed.'

Best Foot Forward was earning a lot of publicity mileage out of its thirty-four-dollars-per-week 'star', and the producers felt they could win even more by encouraging Liza to accept engagements that conflicted with her stage performance. The more professional exposure she attained, the greater the public interest in the show and, since Liza was not technically billed as the star, the producers felt justified in not returning patrons' money during her frequent absences. (Sometimes she 'moonlighted' in the daytime, like appearing at Arnold Constable's Department Store to help celebrate May Day.)

'The show was a success. It was selling out. We could have run for two years,' Whitelaw later complained. But the public, disappointed by Liza's frequent non-appearance, was quick to spread the word that *Best Foot Forward* might well qualify as the rip-off attraction of 1963. Advance sales plummeted. Veronica Lake (replacing Paula Wayne) was added to the cast in a desperate and futile bid to recapture the show's early glamour. It closed on October 13th, 1964, after a seven-month run.

CHAPTER SEVEN

It was actually Judy Garland's daughter, *not* Liza
Minnelli, who had been the unbilled star of *Best Foot
Forward,* and it really mattered little to the general
public that in this off-Broadway revival Liza had
shown promise. The masses were interested only in
stars, and she had not yet found that individuality,
that special quality which makes public personalities.
At present she was a 'six-month' wonder, a curiosity
figure to be forgotten as quickly as the acting appearances of such show business progeny as John Barry-
more, Jnr, Gary Crosby, Jody McCrea, William
Wellman, Jnr, and James Mitchum. She was trivia
when trivia as a commodity could be nothing more
than trivial, and she was 'camp' when camp was still
a quality known and appreciated only by exclusive
circles of chic homosexuals.

Judy saw what was happening and in her own hesitant way she tried to stop it. However, with major
articles on Liza appearing in *Life, The Saturday Evening*

Post, and *Look* magazines, Judy's desire proved to be impossible. Ironically, she would ultimately be accused of attempting to abort Liza's show business career when it was literally stillborn.

Liza had been publicly judged in the light of the dishonesty that *Best Foot Forward* came to represent and, even though she left the production before it closed, the stigma by association remained.

In September, 1963, there was some professional activity in the Liza camp when it was announced that she had signed a three-year contract with the powerful Creative Management Associates, the talent agency that frequently handled Judy. Under-aged Liza thereafter petitioned the local court to be allowed to keep twenty per cent of her future earnings (whatever they might be), but the judge ruled that the minor's pay cheques for the time being were to go to Judy in trust for Liza. By November, however, when no pending performing deals for Liza had been announced, it was rumoured that little Miss Show Business was already a has-been.

Liza's personal life at this time did not speak of much success either. Granted she did have her independence, and she was following a gypsy-like existence, just as she had dreamed about during high school days. She had a new, not too serious escort in young dancer Timmy Everitt and there were stories, true or not, about her being evicted from the Barbizon Hotel for Women, her clothes and possessions confiscated for non-payment of rent, and having to sleep by the fountain in front of the Plaza Hotel and in Central Park before finding a more or less permanent refuge on Paula Wayne's couch. Paula, then as now a perennial 'star of

69

tomorrow' on the summer stock and café circuits, was the leading star in *Best Foot Foward* for a spell.

Liza was certainly not finding much performing work. Though she was unaware of it, what media spots she did obtain with the likes of Keefe Brasselle and Arthur Godfrey on their programmes was due to Judy's influence. Veteran New York radio and TV show interviewers recall that Judy was constantly making personal calls on behalf of her 'baby', soliciting time on their shows.

Not surprisingly, Liza—like Lorna and Joey— earned her best video exposure on Judy's not very successful CBS-TV variety series. That was the Sunday night outing that was foolishly pitted against the popular *Bonanza* series of a rival network. On the November 17th appearance, Liza joined with Soupy Sales, the Brothers Castro, and series regular, Jerry Van Dyke, as Judy's 'guests'. The mother and daughter duets monopolised most of the programme, with Judy and Liza harmonising on *Together*, *We Could Make Such Beautiful Music Together*, *The Best Is Yet to Come*, *Bye Bye Baby*, *Bob White*, and *Let Me Entertain You*. Their two final numbers said a lot about the performers' careers at this juncture: *Two Lost Souls* and *I Will Come Back*.

Liza did return to *The Judy Garland Show* on December 22nd, along with Lorna and Joey, Jack Jones, show regular Mel Torme, and Liza's friend, Timmy Everitt. This time Liza had far fewer opportunities to shine in the spotlight, but rather blended into the background as she joined with her family in a rendition of *Consider Yourself*, then did a trio of *Sleigh Ride* with Jones and Mama, and concluded her contributions to the hour by singing along with the whole crew in *Deck the Halls*.

It was in Los Angeles, in November, just after taping the shows with Mama, that Liza woke one morning to discover '. . . my temperature was raging and my legs felt like wet noodles'. She could not get out of bed and, after three days of hospital tests, the doctors diagnosed her ailment as an hereditary kidney problem.

Liza recovered quickly, but two months later she was stricken again in New York. Judy flew to her side and demanded that she return to California and enjoy a leisurely recuperation. The now much slimmer Liza, however, had just signed for a stock production of *Carnival!* at the Paper Mill Playhouse in Millburn, New Jersey, with options for additional engagements, and she was determined that nothing—or no one— would stop her.

Carnival! was derived from the 1953 MGM hit motion picture *Lili* which had starred Leslie Caron and Mel Ferrer. In its subsequent stage version, with book by Michael Stewart and songs by Bob Merrill, it had featured Anna Maria Alberghetti in a rather pallid adaptation which did little to raise the artistic levels of the 1961 Broadway season. But it offered Liza an ideal performing role as the orphaned carnival girl who brings love to a misanthropic group of Gallic misfits. It also seemed that this part had been tailor-made to Liza's talents.

Judy, understandably, was concerned only with her daughter's health. Strangely, though, that would be the least of the reasons she provided for her subsequent hysterics. She ranted and raged. She threatened legal action against Liza and against the producers of the show and she bombarded the press with stories that Liza would not—could not—perform.

Pat Hipp, then a press agent for the 1,200-seat Paper Mill Playhouse, remembers those times and she recalls also how the producers signed Liza because they wanted a future star and one who would not be too expensive for their budget. Miss Hipp, telling of that engagement for the readership of the *Asbury Park Press*, recalled that she had been told to sell the show subtly, sneaking in references to Judy so that Liza, still very much determined to make her success on her own, would not be offended by the news copy.

'We were selling lots of tickets for the month's run,' Pat Hipp wrote. 'And then whammo, Judy Garland's lawyer called. She was pulling Liza out of the show.'

'Too young,' Judy was quoted as saying. 'Much too young to be in the theatre. Not now—and maybe never,' she is said to have added.

'Then began the coast-to-coast calls,' recalls Pat. 'The begging, the hysterics. We didn't know from minute to minute if we had a show.'

Liza, too, was at her nerves' ends and justifiably so. 'She seemed to be held together by snapping rubber bands, rather than cartilage,' observed the beleaguered press girl.

Throughout this tense time of rehearsal, however, Liza was a thorough professional. Never late. She was always polite and constantly watchful. Yet somehow she seemed too shy and insecure for the position in which she had been suddenly placed.

'I had certainly noted her intensity,' Pat Hipp wrote. 'Her concentration during rehearsals was spooky. But a star? All I knew was that she was hyper-kinetic and that Judy Garland had left us all wringing wet with nerves.

'Rehearsals were going badly and the cast's morale was shot. Judy was pulling the rug out from under us . . . then just as suddenly as Judy had started making trouble, she was stopped. Vincente Minnelli, we were told, had persuaded her that Liza should have her chance.

'So we opened.'

Opening night was a sell-out occasion.

'Liza walked on,' Pat vividly recalls. 'How truly a waif she was. She'd been crying backstage before the performance. She was gorgeous. Not in the sense of beautiful, but of real, of lost, of heartbreaking, of needing. And her voice reached out and loved us. It was beautiful.'

One of those attending the opening night was *Newsday*'s Mike McGrady who reported, 'The comparisons to Judy Garland are inevitable—the tremulous voice, the respect for the lyric, the wide eyes, the clenching hands, the eyebrows never still. Yet, by the time she sings her second number, *Yes, My Heart*, the applause belongs to her alone; from that point on, forget to make the comparisons.'

The show was a smash. No more was heard from Judy. She never came to any of the performances in Millburn or at subsequent dates Liza played along the Eastern seaboard.

When it was over, Pat Hipp was simply relieved that an unpleasant experience had finally come to a happy ending.

'I hadn't the vaguest notion of what lay ahead for Liza,' she wrote. 'She was a skinny kid who cried a lot and performed superbly and she was a pain in the neck because of the hell her mother put us through.'

CHAPTER EIGHT

Liza does not cry any more, at least not when people can see her. It has been said that when her mother died she wept just once, and that was when coming from the airport, where Judy's grotesquely made-up corpse had arrived unceremoniously in a corrugated cardboard casket.

She had been toughened. Toughened by her mother. Toughened by the exploiters and the opportunists who imagined her to be an easy 'take', in court or out, because she is Liza Minnelli and, in the public sense, so very vulnerable.

She is vulnerable, too, in a private sense and to her friends it is one of her most appealing qualities. But Liza does not like her vulnerability. It is the side of herself she does not wish the public to recognise because, still, she does not want to become another Judy Garland.

Sympathy is not Liza's business. It never was. She yearns to be loved and she wants to demonstrate her love. But on her very own terms. She is a woman of the year 2001 in the twentieth-century world: the human being who has tried and, to an extent, succeeded in being superhuman.

Liza tries to live outside her emotional skin, outside herself. She will programme her emotions and her life as strictly as she plots her performance on stage. She will be the perfect non-being: the ultimate body machine.

In 1970, in an interview for *After Dark* magazine with her friend Craig Zadan, Liza confided, 'The only thing that really scares me in life is the realisation of the innumerable possibilities of pain.'

'The human body scares me,' Liza continued. 'People's insides. Sometimes I think, "My God, the whole thing that's allowing me to feel, my heart, is just a thing that's pumping. What if it stops? Do I have to stop?" '

'People seem so vulnerable,' she added. 'It really frightens me when I'm not in total control.'

By 1974, Liza seemed to have found the pattern for a controlled existence. In an extraordinary talk with Barbara Walters on the NBC-TV *Today* show, in January, just before her engagement at the Winter Garden Theatre, Liza exclaimed, 'There's two things I can't bear: pity and depression. I don't have time for it. It's not in my schedule.'

The usually unflappable hostess of the *Today* show seemed momentarily nonplussed by the intensity of Liza's remarks. But Barbara Walters also is an 'in' person. She knows more about the private lives of celebrities than the general public and she had heard rumours about the possible abortion that Liza is alleged to have had after her mid-1973 British interlude with Peter Sellers.

Barbara, subtly, brought up the subject of family and marriage. Liza, taken off guard, had to respond to the interviewer's questions in a manner approximating honesty and humanity.

'Really, there's a certain standard every woman has to go by,' she said. 'And that is . . . uh, it's taught from the time when you are a kid. You have a doll and, you know, it's a normal thing to have . . .' Liza paused briefly, then hastily added, 'to marry and to work.

'It's very normal and sane. I can't go by those standards,' she said. 'And I used to go crazy 'cause it would make me guilty and I'd say "Ah, what am I doing? I'm going on stage every night. It's not normal." It would panic me, and I suddenly thought, "Hold it, I can't . . . I gotta get a whole different set of rules." Otherwise, I'm going to become a neurotic and that's not in my schedule either.'

Liza believes that her business is fantasy and so she seems to have made her life a fantasy too. Song writer Fred Ebb, the Svengali she credits with transforming her from Judy Garland's daughter into Liza Minnelli, Superstar, has built a legend around her, and Liza, literally, is living up to the legend. She has found her public image in the original songs that Ebb and John Kander have written for her.   From the playful egoisms of *Liza with a Z* and the self-deprecating egomania of *Exactly Like Me* to the dehumanised paranoia of *I'm One of the Smart Ones*, songs so distinctly tailored to the Liza image that no one else can or does sing them, she has created within herself the fantasies that make the songs into autobiographical statements.

Reality, again, is something Liza rises above.

CHAPTER NINE

'Got it figured, got it planned,' Liza sings in one of the Kander–Ebb songs, *I'm One of the Smart Ones*. Liza was not one of the 'smart ones' in 1964.

Despite the success of the *Carnival!* engagement, her career was not progressing well. Relieved of the pressures of that play date, Liza's subsequent performances began to suffer in contrast. The problem again, and this time indirectly, was her mother.

Liza was determined to establish her own identity, and her voice, she felt, was too much like Judy's. 'I tried so hard not to sound like her that, uh, I wasn't singing well at all. It wasn't like anything . . . I was floundering out there in front of everybody which was, uh, interesting.'

She tried her hand at straight acting, appearing with Chester Morris at the Bucks County Playhouse in *Time Out for Ginger*, the Broadway comedy that would, in 1965 under the title *Billie*, become an unsatisfactory movie comedy vehicle for Patty Duke. Liza's main memory of that engagement in Pennsylvania was that veteran Morris never appeared on stage, or anywhere, without first literally bathing himself in Colgate 100. The effect, to Liza, was staggering. But then Liza's penchant for imbibing well-seasoned Italian foods, highly spiced with garlic, and her disdain for any breath refreshers other than chewing gum may have proved equally staggering to the fast-talking Morris.

A more pleasant experience was touring that summer with lanky Elliott Gould in an edition of the off-Broadway perennial, *The Fantasticks*, a musical vehicle that Liza adored. Like Liza, Gould then was something more than an unknown but less than a star, his career having been eclipsed by the spectacular rise of his wife of that time, Barbra Streisand. Liza and Gould had much in common and they established an immediate offstage rapport.

At about this time, too, Liza discovered that she was not earning enough to cover her costs and that she was several thousand dollars into debt and approaching bankruptcy. At eighteen she found herself in the position of becoming possibly one of the youngest debtors in America. Like mother, like daughter, the cynics said, but Liza gave her lawyer power of attorney to manage her finances and settle bills. Later she would come under the financial control of high-powered business manager Martin Bregman.

Even though Liza was obtaining work in the various media, the pay scale was obviously not enough for her standard of living. In the autumn she had even made a bid to branch out as a dramatic television actress. Her agent had sold Liza's acting services to the producers of the New York-filmed TV series *Mr Broadway*, starring Craig Stevens. She was hired to play Minnie, the aspiring opera singer niece of former hoodlum Eduardo Ciannelli in the *Nightingale for Sale* episode of the NBC programme. It would be televised on October 24th but Liza would receive little attention from the critics for her on camera contributions, and no more guest-starring stints like that turned up, or, if they did, the price was too low to have any saving grace.

Besides her money problems, Liza was still feeling somewhat hostile towards Judy because of the *Carnival!* fracas, and so she was surprised when Mama invited her to London in September. It soon became apparent that Judy was in one of her 'wonderful Mama' periods again, but this time she overplayed her hand. She tried to be doting mother, confiding sister, and matchmaker. Liza was not having any of it until the day Judy asked her to co-star, not merely appear, with her at the London Palladium.

Liza was overwhelmed by her mother's 'spontaneous' offer. 'It was her first acknowledgment that I might really be talented,' the still bitter daughter later remarked.

It was the wrong time for a mother–daughter public love-in. Judy had not fully recovered from a mysterious ailment she had developed in Hong Kong and, in late September, she was again hospitalised in London. Her voice was frayed, her senses numbed. Still, apparently, she felt she had to make this gesture for Liza.

The joint concert was scheduled for November 8. It was a complete sell-out within two days of the initial announcement and a second performance was quickly added.

Liza, meanwhile, had been commuting between

London and New York and had auditioned, not too successfully, for a Broadway show, *Flora, the Red Menace*. It did not look, then, as though she would get the part, but she had met Fred Ebb, one of the show's composers. He had given her confidence in her own abilities, in her power to hold an audience and to create, individually, the kind of magic and rapport that Liza hitherto had considered solely her mother's domain.

It was inevitable that the Palladium concerts would prove to be a duel between mother and daughter. Judy, certainly, was unaware of this before the first performance and Liza, though probably blind to the ultimate consequences, was determined to prove herself. She was going to match the unmatchable, to surpass the unsurpassable. And she did it.

The Palladium concerts did not make Liza a superstar, for the British audience was primarily her mother's, but they did make her a major star. Without this appearance, it seems unlikely that she would have had the opportunity for Broadway fame and received the Tony award in *Flora, the Red Menace*.

For Judy, however, the Palladium appearance would prove the end of her reign as the *grande dame* of American superstars. She was playing *A Star Is Born* for the second time, but now the roles were reversed and Judy did not have a convenient ocean in which to make a graceful, climactic exit.

Though Judy would never publicly comment on the Palladium engagement, her daughter would not be so restrained.

'When I was a little girl and had jumped up on stage to dance while she sang, it was an unrehearsed, amateurish, spontaneous thing,' Liza said. 'Working with her was something else. I'll never be afraid to perform with anyone ever again after that terrifying experience.'

Judy, it seemed, used every showmanship trick she knew to upstage and outperform her daughter at the first of the two Palladium concerts and, at the end, she virtually pushed Liza angrily off stage.

'Mama, at this point, suddenly realised that she had a grown-up daughter; that she wasn't a kid herself any more,' is the way Liza explains the traumatic incident, adding sympathetically, 'I'm sure this happens with almost any mother and daughter. It happened to my mother in front of eight thousand people.'

Many of those present saw the situation differently. Liza, they felt, had deliberately provoked her mother, challenged her, and Judy foolishly accepted. The evidence supplied by the LP recordings of the concerts reinforces this view.

The performance began innocuously with Judy and Liza duetting a show tune. Then Judy soloed weakly with *The Man that Got Away* from *A Star Is Born*. It was usually one of her show-stoppers.

Liza then set the tone for the drama that followed with an incredible rendition of the oldie *Who's Sorry Now?* It was strictly a Liza Minnelli version of the song, sung in a manner that would have been beyond her mother's capabilities. Beginning easily in a nicely jazzy vein that echoed Ella Fitzgerald, the artist her father had told Liza to exemplify in learning how to sing, Liza then built slowly and subtly to a shrieking hostility directed clearly at her mother.

'You . . . YOU had your way. NOW you must PAY,' wailed Liza.

The number brought Liza the first really big ovation of the evening and the battle was on.

Even with this triumph, she was not satisfied. She had to continue pounding at her vulnerable mother. In their duet of *It All Depends on You*, Liza felt it requisite to make her own interpolation: 'You're to blame, MOTHER, for what I do.' The way she pronounced 'mother', it could have been 'mother-fucker' and it was probably the only time in her life that Liza referred to Mama as 'mother'.

By the second show, Judy had given up trying to compete with frenetic, vindictive Liza. She was so exhausted and in such bad voice that she could not even get through *Over the Rainbow* and asked the empathising audience to sing it for her. They did.

Liza, however, was still not content. She had to portray herself as the victim of the evening. 'She became very competitive with me. I wasn't Liza. I was another woman in the same spotlight,' she whined. 'It was just too hard for me to try to cope. And it was her night. I wanted it to be her night.'

Ironically, the BBC's television taping of the concert (shown in England on December 9th, and much later in the United States) captured little of the flavour of the actual event. 'They cut a two-and-a-half hour concert down to an hour,' complained Liza, 'and they left in all the applause and the hugging and cut most of the numbers.'

According to Liza, 'Mama's competitiveness disappeared immediately after the Palladium performance, and she fell into a period of unparalleled motherhood with me.' This included finding a husband for Liza.

'I have met the most divine boy,' Judy told her daughter. 'You two have the same crazy sense of humour.'

The boy was Peter Woolnough-Allen, an Australian folk singer in his early twenties who had a 'brother' act with Chris Bell that was called 'Chris and Peter Allen'. Judy had seen the Allen 'brothers' performing in Tokyo and had hired them for her own act, mainly, Liza believes, as a device for bringing herself and Peter together.

It worked. Liza was immediately attracted to Peter and a month after they met, soon after the Palladium concert, they became engaged.

As Liza recalls the 'momentous' occasion, she was with Mama, Chris, Peter, and Judy's current beau, Mark Herron (then alleged to be prospective husband number four) at Trader Vic's in London and they were all '. . . pretty high on those exotic drinks they serve'. While Judy was in the powder room and Chris was making a phone call, Peter asked Liza to 'go steady' with him.

'To ask Liza to do that, you have to be engaged,' Herron is supposed to have said.

'All right,' replied Peter. 'Let's be engaged then.'

Liza, stunned by the suddenness and casualness of it all, just shrugged. Judy cried with joy and Peter ran to his nearby flat and returned with a tiny diamond ring that he had formerly worn on his little finger. They were now officially engaged.

'I was uncertain and afraid,' Liza recalls.

The next day she had to fly to New York to audition, again, for *Flora, the Red Menace*.

CHAPTER TEN

'I remember this shy, awkward girl coming into the room,' says Fred Ebb of his first meeting with Liza Minnelli. 'She looked awful, like Raggedy Ann. Everything was just a little torn and a little soiled. She just sat there and stared at me, and I stared back.'

It was shortly after Liza's closing in *Best Foot Forward*, and Ebb was captivated by this strange, yet appealing girl. He played some of the songs he had written for *Flora, the Red Menace* and Liza knew immediately that she wanted to be Flora.

'Whenever there's something I want, really want,' Liza has said, 'I persevere until I get it. I really hounded Fred and George Abbott, and later I did the same thing with Alan Pakula for *The Sterile Cuckoo*. It took me three years to get *that* part.'

Ebb did not require too much convincing. He sensed a magical quality in the bizarre girl, the potential to be a really tremendous performer, and he soon began providing her with musical guidance. Liza's first solo LP album, *Liza! Liza!*, released in December, 1964, featured two Ebb–Kander songs. One was *If I Were In Your Shoes* and the other, *Maybe This Time*, a number initially written for Kaye Ballard's nightclub act, but which would become indelibly associated with Liza. The Capitol Records' disc also included a song by Marvin Hamlisch, *The Travellin' Life*. (When Capitol released their first Liza album, they were so uncertain of the public's reception to the new vocalist that all their advertisements trotted out the girl's artistic pedigree, dragging Judy and Minnelli into the packaged product by proxy. The album did not sell very well.)

Under Ebb's deft tutelage, Liza soon began to find a distinctive style, a style that joined form and substance to the energy of her momentous Palladium performance, particularly apparent in her rendition of *Who's Sorry Now?* with its premonitions of the drive and powers that, years later, she would instil in her delivery of the title song from *Cabaret*.

Though Ebb believed that Liza would make the deal on-stage Flora, septuagenarian George Abbott, who wrote the book with Robert Russell and who had been signed to direct, had different feelings on the matter.

The day of her first audition for Abbott, Liza waited in the wings of the rehearsal hall for her turn to 'show her stuff' to the tough director. Marvin Hamlisch was in the pit, set to play for Liza's stage test.

After what seemed an endless wait, the stage assistant walked out on to the stage, and announced to Abbott and the others gathered in the orchestra, 'Liza

Minnelli, *Best Foot Forward*, *The Ed Sullivan Show*, Judy Garland and Vincente Minnelli's daughter.'

Liza then came on to the starkly lit stage and just as she began her first audition tune, she heard Abbott saying to an associate, 'This is a waste of time.' He hardly listened to her run-through, thinking her a pest and, having seen her in *Best Foot Forward* (a show he had directed for its initial Broadway run), he was convinced that she was without sufficient talent. He later remarked to a co-worker, 'She's not right for the part. She's not what I had in mind and I don't think she'll be able to carry it.'

But Liza felt differently. 'I wanted to do *Flora* so badly that I just kept auditioning,' said Liza, who each time she talked to the press increased the number of actual auditions she endured for the part. 'I just kept going back until they couldn't get rid of me.' During this period, Liza was also auditioning for *Roman Holiday*, a musical based on the Audrey Hepburn–Gregory Peck motion picture that never got beyond the planning stages.

Finally, in Miami, veteran showman Abbott capitulated to a determined Liza. He had wanted Eydie Gorme but she was unavailable and it was a matter of either accepting Liza or cancelling the production.

And so *Flora* went into rehearsals. Bob Dishy, the fuzzy-haired comedian who had scored as a member of the Second City improvisational gang and was later a part of television's *This was the Week that Was* troupe, was set to play Liza's zany co-star. (Offstage, Liza would become very 'chummy' with Dishy and the twosome would often be seen together prowling around Greenwich Village haunts or sampling spaghetti at some low-price Italian restaurant.) Mary Louise Wilson and Cathryn Damon, two very striking actresses, were hired as supporting leads to Liza. When rehearsals got under way, Liza's eagerness and indefatigible energy impressed even Abbott. I've never seen anyone take direction that fast since, Helen Hayes,' he said.

Publicly, it was being touted how well Liza was responding to the demands of a pivotal lead role in a Broadway musical. Privately, everyone connected with *Flora* did their best to keep as quiet as possible Liza's rather unconventional hygienic regime, which branded her as a very 'different' Broadway leading lady. Many of those involved with *Flora* maintain that it was Fred Ebb, like a virtual lion tamer, who transformed the raw, undisciplined Liza into a totally new being, professionally and personally, making her aware of facts of life that most girls would have learned from their mothers at a much earlier time.

Producer Hal Prince decided to give *Flora* only a modified out-of-town try-out. It debuted on Saturday, April 3rd, at the Shubert Theatre in New Haven. 'Amiable but unexciting,' was the verdict of the town's critics, and so the jumbled show went through much revamping before it opened at the Colonial Theatre on Wednesday, April 14th. *Variety*'s Hub reporter was on hand to record that Liza 'has intriguing stage presence, a good voice, and a captivating manner'. However, audiences were apathetic to the show itself, and too many of the theatre patrons were voicing the standard that had long been the bane of Liza's existence: 'Gee, she looks and sings so much like Judy . . . but Judy would have done the part so much better . . . why does she copy Judy's every mannerism . . . ? did you notice the way she moves her head *just like Judy*?'

And the real-life Judy was not making it any easier for Liza either. There was at least one occasion during the *Flora* rehearsals in New York when a distraught Manhattan hotel manager had to call to alert Liza that Miss Garland was indisposed and in her delirium had locked both Lorna and Joey outside on the hotel suite terrace in freezing February weather. A very tense Liza was forced to go to her sister and brother's rescue. It was thus somewhat of a relief for Liza to go out of town with *Flora*, despite the demands of constant show revisions, performing, and engaging in the seemingly endless rounds of press conferences and interviews.

As with *Best Foot Forward* there was constant speculation whether Judy would actually show up at Liza's opening night on Broadway, and if she actually did, would she be in condition to act the proper parent. (It evolved that Judy, enmeshed in another round of her love–hate relationship with Liza, would make is to the cast party where she seemed to have a better time than Liza. Vincente would be there too, smiling throughout the evening, the perfect picture of a pleased papa.)

Meanwhile the fate of the very expensive *Flora* was becoming obvious. It was doomed to failure.

'To say the least, it was a disaster,' Ebb said afterwards. 'It just didn't work. The book was sort of strange and the score sounded like a series of revue numbers because it wasn't connected by the strength of the libretto.'

Flora, the Red Menace, as it was distilled for the stage, told of an impressionable (and how!) young miss who graduates from the New York High School of Commercial Art in the midst of the Depression. She is soon persuaded by her impoverished beau (Bob Dishy) to become a Communist enthusiast. By the end of the improbable tale, which was far more biting in the original book form, she can exclaim jubilantly that she is neither a Communist, nor a capitalist. 'I am me,' she sings. Down comes the final curtain.

The spring of 1965 was a season of flopping musical shows. *Baker Street, Bajour, Do I Hear a Waltz, I Had a Ball, Roar of the Grease Paint—the Smell of the Crowd*, and *What Makes Sammy Run?* were all inflicted on Broadway theatregoers, making most patrons wish they had bought tickets to see over again such long-running hits as *Funny Girl, Fiddler on the Roof*, or *Hello, Dolly!*

Flora, the Red Menace, after many last-minute alterations which saw Liza's two big dance numbers cut from the show, along with some of her favourite lyrics in the musical, finally premièred on Tuesday evening, May 11th, 1965, at the Alvin Theatre. It received unanimously ambivalent reviews: three somewhat favourable, two yes-and-no statements, and one pan.

As for Liza, the press was not all that sure. One aisle sitter insisted that she was 'this year's Barbra Streisand'. Howard Taubman of the *New York Times* reported, 'The voice is not yet distinctive, but she can keep the rhythm pounding and driving and can belt out the climactic tones. . . . She is going to be a popular singer, all right.' Norman Nadel of the *New York*

World Telegram and Sun wrote a response to the question that was on everyone's mind. 'Miss Minnelli has established beyond a shadow of a doubt that she is herself and no second-edition Judy.' Nadel continued, 'The girl has the face of a startled rabbit—wide, watchful eyes and an apprehensive upper lip. There is something charmingly gauche about her toe-in stance, and the way she charges into situations, as if her physical momentum would overcome her inner trepidation. The aspect of blinded innocence and courage make her perfect as the girl who can be talked into joining the party and eventually strong-arming her way out.'

The most lavish praise came from *Time* magazine which said, 'At nineteen, Liza Minnelli is a star-to-be, a performer of arresting presence who does not merely occupy the stage but fills it.' The most devastating review, as far as Liza was concerned, came from *Newsweek* magazine, and it so upset the girl that she redoubled her efforts to improve her stage performance in any manner possible. Said the blistering magazine reviewer, '. . . her voice is thin, her movements stiff, her presence wobbly and uncertain.'

The public's response to *Flora* was as non-committal as that of the critics. Regardless of Liza's snappy presence in the show, her marquee lure was not drawing sufficient patrons to fill the 1,344-seat Broadway theatre and on Saturday, July 24th, 1965, at the end of its eleventh week, and after eighty-seven performances, the show closed at an estimated operating loss of 389,000 dollars of its 400,000-dollar investment. A Tony Award for Liza in June, as Best Musical Actress of the Year, had failed to boost its box-office receipts (during the show's last week it was grossing 19,000 dollars out of a potential 74,172-dollar take). Nor did the original cast album (recorded May 9th) for RCA Victor alert possible ticket buyers of the show's actual scope.

Liza's Antoinette Perry (Tony) prize came as a surprise to many but, considering that the other nominees that season were Elizabeth Allen (*Do I Hear a Waltz*), Nancy Dussault (*Bajour*), and Inga Swenson (*Baker Street*), all performers in equal flop shows, it was not such a strange choice after all.

By the time that *Flora* closed, its producer, Hal Prince along with Fred Ebb and John Kander, was already deeply involved in *Cabaret*. It was a show that Liza dearly loved. Some of the songs, she claimed, had been written with her in mind. She believed herself ideal for the role of Sally Bowles and she was determined to have it.

Joe Masteroff, writer of the book for the musical adaptation of the John Van Druten play *I Am a Camera*, based in turn on Christopher Isherwood's *Berlin Stories*, was adamant in insisting, however, that Sally had to be played by a British girl and Prince, along with producing associate Ruth Mitchell, backed him up. There could be no place in *Cabaret* for Liza Minnelli.

Liza, then as now, did not accept defeat. It is not permitted . . . it is not allowed. If she could not play Sally on Broadway, she would still be Sally. She would let the world know that she, Liza Minnelli, *was* Sally Bowles.

Liza set about making her life a public audition for *Cabaret*. She would make them notice her rapport with

Sally. Naïvely, she even thought she could make the public demand that she be Sally. Explaining her unconventional living arrangements with Tanya Everett, an attractive young actress then playing one of Tevye's daughters in Hal Prince's *Fiddler on the Roof* and also dee-jaying at a local discotheque, Liza said in dialogue that was pure Sally Bowles, 'We have one apartment on the West Side and one on the East Side, and we split the rents. . . . The point is that we each need an apartment and if I'm working it's a hassle to get from the East Side to Broadway on matinee days . . . the traffic is incredible. So I sleep in the West Side apartment the nights before matinee days. But usually,' she rattled on, 'we stay at whichever apartment is convenient and another advantage is that you don't get sick of your roommate.' Tenants of the Westerly, the high-rise luxury apartment building on Eighth Avenue at Fifty-Fifth Street, were used to unique situations in that anything-goes dwelling, but many had to admit that the Minnelli–Everett household was perhaps the strangest of all.

While Liza was baffling herself, the press, and the public about her 'home' life, she also insisted on convincing the world that she was still very much in the running for the *Cabaret* lead. Although in reality she auditioned only once for the musical, the number, according to Liza, soon worked itself up to fourteen tries for the Sally Bowles role. Liza's barnstorming tactics, however, did not work this time. The producers stuck to their original intention to cast a British girl, Jill Haworth, and so Liza found herself living a role that could not, it seemed, be hers.

Always practical, Liza soon found the solution. If

there was one Sally, there must be others and Liza located her in Pookie Adams, the heroine of John Nichols' novel *The Sterile Cuckoo* It would take her three years to get the role of Pookie and it would cost her the lead in the Broadway musical *Promises, Promises,* but it would make her a major motion picture star and it would earn her an Academy Award nomination. And Christopher Isherwood, the man who had known the real Sally Bowles and had immortalised her in *Berlin Stories,* would see *The Sterile Cuckoo* film in London in 1969 and he would be enchanted by Liza Minnelli.

'You know,' he confided to a friend, 'that girl is a lot like Sally.'

Liza has always maintained that she is not playing herself on stage or in motion pictures. And, of course, she is right. She does, however, seem constantly to be living the roles she is playing. The girl who was so compulsively gabby, so charming a prevaricator, and so needful of love and attention when Pookie and Sally were uppermost in her career mind, would become reclusive and fiercely independent as Junie Moon. Likewise, as Liza had been frumpy as Flora, she would, in turn, be the incredibly individualistic stage superstar known as Liza Minnelli, wafting from identity to identity, creating new personalities, each an old friend, with chameleon-like alacrity.

The real Liza may lay buried beneath, hidden even from herself, but most definitely hidden by deliberation. Obviously, it is true that there are doors she does not want opened, not just yet. Maybe never.

CHAPTER ELEVEN

There was a new element now in Liza's life—public adulation. She had always been in the public eye, but it had been her mother in the spotlight and it had been her mother who had been the ardent object of fan hysteria. Now, it was happening to Liza and she did not like it. She wanted to communicate with her audiences. She did not wish to be a receptacle for their cornucopia of emotions.

'Fans!' she once said with unmasked distaste. 'They put their hands all over you. They touch you and push you. And the old women look so fragile, but when they grab your arm they leave bruise marks.'

Liza wanted stardom, wanted it badly, but on her own terms. She might become a public personality, but she had to remain a private person.

'It's a matter of you can't live up to anyone but yourself. That's it,' she said, 'and you're not supposed to live up to anybody but yourself.'

'I wouldn't live with the hopes that people will say,

"That's our girl." Well, I'm not a lot of people's girl . . . I'm my own girl.'

'No, I'm not saying, "Screw you," ' Liza has said in explaining her attitude towards her audiences. 'What I'm saying is that I do what I do, the best I can, and I hope you like it.'

'Come with me and enjoy . . .'—this is the essence of Liza's public appeal. Her approach could never be personified by the wish, 'Come to me and worship.' Liza wants the respect that comes with achievement, not the adulation that is automatically showered upon public idols.

Idols, it seems, are made to be crushed and then, sometimes, rebuilt. She has seen it happen many times with her mother, and that route was not for her. Liza would not be crushed . . . not ever.

Liza made it clear from the start that she was, and would remain, a winner. And Liza, unlike her mother, would have *her* Oscar. Winners like this have to be tough, and Liza readily admits it.

'But,' she adds, 'I think the toughness is there only when needed, not something I've adopted as myself. A lot of people who are tough on the outside are marshmallow on the inside, and I'm the opposite. It's merely self-preservation.'

Her friends agree. Liza has always been selective in her choice of friends and intimates and, usually, when she establishes a close relationship it remains close no matter what may happen. (And with Liza a lot is always happening.)

In her friendships Liza gives rather than demands. It is because of her that Marvin Hamlisch earned his first major break in musical circles as assistant musical director for the Broadway production of *Funny Girl*, and this before Liza was established as an important star.

And while Liza owes much to Fred Ebb, the talented man who moulded her adult career and her current image, she in turn has lifted him from the level of a respected but mostly publicity-anonymous lyricist into something of a legend, a modern Svengali with an instinct for knowing where it is at and who it is with. Because of Liza, Ebb is now considered one of the most 'in' persons in Broadway's elite circles. It was probably because of Ebb, however, that Liza's engagement to Peter Allen turned into an uncertain courtship that lasted some two and a half years before their actual marriage.

'I hated Peter's friends and he disliked mine,' Liza later recalled. 'The only person I loved and trusted was Fred Ebb. I'm sure Peter misunderstood my devotion to Fred, just as I distrusted his coterie of acquaintances.'

Then, too, Vincente Minnelli objected to Peter as a prospective husband for his daughter, publicly protesting that they were each too young for so serious an emotional step. Even Judy was now having second thoughts. She did not approve of Peter's life style. And so it was easy for Liza to prolong the engagement. Besides, marriage was not in Sally Bowles' vision of life and Liza, at this time, was very much in her 'Sally' period. Later, she would learn that the *real* Sally had eventually married and had children.

Liza's career, however, could not be postponed. She was becoming 'hot'. She was on the move and she had to sustain the snowballing momentum. She was a star, but she wanted to be a bigger star. Fred Ebb and John Kander were toying with the idea of a new musical to star Liza and to be called *Tomato Pie* (it would never come to pass), but meantime under the guidance of Ebb she developed a nightclub act.

The test opening out of town was at the Shoreham Hotel's Blue Room in Washington, DC, in mid-September. She had finally got it all together. The new Liza was ready to make her stunning debut.

She had a smashing wardrobe for the occasion: a gown hemmed two inches above her knees, with its Mondrian patchwork design glittering with red sequins and white beads. There was a blue chiffon number for the dancing segments, and for the finale she would wear a Grecian-style white affair. Although she carried no contingent of musicians or conductor for her act (which was unusual for such a prestige engagement), she did bring along two dancing partners: short and plump Neil Schwartz and tall and lean Robert Fitch.

The act and Liza were a singular smash. She performed some eighteen numbers including *Gypsy in My Soul*, *Too Marvellous*, *Everbyody Loves My Baby*, did a routine which she tagged—thanks to Ebb's suggestion —*Songs I Taught My Mother*, and closed her performance with *Sing Happy* from *Flora, the Red Menace*.

The audience reaction was more than anyone could have anticipated. 'She put the full house opening night audience on its feet, which is very unusual in the huge, sophisticated Blue Room. She is one of only two or three performers who have received a standing ovation . . . on opening night in the last fifteen years,' reported the *Variety* correspondent.

Liza was indeed amazed herself at the customers' response to her show. 'Oh, I can't believe it,' she cried out with glee. 'You are too good to me.' Truly she had been an apt pupil in learning the effective humility act which was so much a part of Judy's onstage routine.

Despite her Washington success (one critic wrote, 'Her songs, dances and patter are magnificent, written and staged to make the most out of her remarkable talent and personality'), the nation's capital cannot be considered the entertainment big time. She had to play in the Big Apple if she were to be really on top. At any rate, she had proved that she could hold the attention of demanding cabaret crowds. Above all, she had demonstrated that she had that distinctive personality and individual 'pzzazz' that characterises the entertainment greats.

'I'm not just Judy Garland's daughter,' Liza pronounced at the time, 'I'm Liza Minnelli. I've always known that.' Now that Washington knew it, too, she was ready to let New York discover what—and who— Liza Minnelli really was.

However, she first had a commitment to ABC-TV network to co-star with Cyril Ritchard, Vic Damone, and The Animals in a musical special, *The Dangerous Christmas of Red Riding Hood*. The show, which could have been cute, proved to be a bore when televised on Sunday, November 28th, 1965. Jules Styne and Bob Merrill had provided the songs, with Robert Emmett serving as librettist. Everyone and everything was straining to be so oh so cute, and it just was not. Ritchard tried to be tongue-in-cheek debonair as Lone T. Wolf who had been ostracised for social climbing and

98

relates how Lillian Hood (Liza) was responsible. Jack Gould (*New York Times*) summed up the mish-mash when he penned of Liza that she '. . . brought an earnest sincerity to her singing and playing, but her limited resources in both were a handicap in raising the program to a gay and tuneful lark'. Liza had yet to develop her penchant for off-handed comedy.

A far more successful occasion was her opening at the Plaza Hotel's prestigious Persian Room on February 9th, 1966, and she was a hit with critics and audiences alike. Her engagement was a sell-out. Once again, she presented the audience with a craftily arranged entertainment package. There was variety in her garb: a backless black gown, a simple school dress, and an interlude in which she sported sexy tights.

Leonard Harris, then with the *New York World Telegram and Sun*, summed it up best in a manner that was less gushy than some of his more enthusiastically superlative-tossing reviewing cohorts. More importantly, he was far more incisive in his judgment of Liza the nightclub *chanteuse*. 'Liza Minnelli', he wrote, 'proved she could sock the stuffings out of a song, dance beautifully for a singer—and even pretty well for a dancer—and turn on that built-in spotlight that is the *sine qua non* of the cabaret performer.'

Despite the bulk of raves for her Persian Room stand, there was one alien voice in the crowd of four-estaters which particularly irked Liza. The reporter from *Newsweek* magazine insisted, 'But all the slick Las Vegas arrangements couldn't get her to sing *He's My Guy* or *They Wouldn't Believe Me* as if she meant it. A girl has to have lived a little to sing about the seamy sides of life and love.' With her traumatic background, it seemed almost impossible that any 'with it' person could make such a statement concerning Liza. For a girl of her relatively young age, she had done a hell of a lot of living between 1946 and 1966.

Newsweek and a few sympathisers to one side, Liza was now a genuine cabaret star. Her recordings were selling fine, if not spectacularly so, and her December, 1966, Capitol release, *There Is a Time*, would receive the Best Album of the Year Award from *Hi-Fi Stereo Review* magazine. Ironically, when she became a genuine superstar her LPs/cassettes/tapes would not sell so well. The record-buying public, predominantly teenaged, wanted artists with single hits and Liza was strictly an album artist. And at that, Liza was always far more vibrant to see and hear, than to just listen to on the record player.

The next step, obviously, in Liza's quest for public immortality was the motion pictures. Only the movies were not interested. The moviemakers—or at least, one moviemaker—were, but the people who produce and distribute films were firm in insisting that Liza was not, and could not be, a movie star. Maybe in musicals some day, but musicals were then dead at the box office, so it was 'Come back in five years, kid. Maybe then, we'll want singers rather than actresses.'

Liza, at this time, had her heart firmly set on playing Pookie Adams. She did not care whether *The Sterile Cuckoo* was done as a film or a play. It was the role that mattered and Alan J. Pakula owned the screen rights. So it would be the movies, which was certainly the best step forward anyway.

New York-born Pakula, up to that point, had been

highly successful as a producer with Robert Mulligan directing in the Pakula–Mulligan film packages: *To Kill a Mockingbird, Love with a Proper Stranger*, and to a lesser extent with *Inside Daisy Clover*.* The Yale University-bred Pakula, who had once been involved with a string of arty stage flops (*Comes a Day, Laurette, There Must Be a Pony*), now wanted to direct films and *The Sterile Cuckoo* was to be his initial big screen venture. The now defunct National General Pictures would finance and distribute.

Liza convinced Pakula that she *was* Pookie, that she was the only actress who could play Pookie and bring it off successfully. He told executives at National General that he wished Liza to play the role. They were incredulous. Pakula's talent as a director was as yet unproven and he frivolously wanted to use this 'singer', this awkward, ugly girl. Absolutely not! Elizabeth Hartman, who had just earned an Academy Award nomination for her performance as the blind girl in *A Patch of Blue*, could play the role and the budget would be approved, She wanted to play the role. So did Patty Duke. Maybe Tuesday Weld. But Liza Minnelli . . . never!

Finally, it was made clear to the obstinate Pakula that either he accept one of the actresses approved by the company or the production would be cancelled. In a display of integrity rare in the Hollywood community, Pakula asserted that the picture would be

*In the 1970s Pakula admitted to a New York reporter that as much as he admired Natalie Wood's performance in this 1965 story about Hollywood, it would have been a far sounder screen version if he had been aware of Liza at the time and used her for the pivotal screen part.

made with Liza Minnelli or not at all. The production was cancelled. The Pakula–Mulligan team then turned their attention to *Up the Down Staircase* (1967), which would star Sandy Dennis, Eileen Heckart, and Jean Stapleton.

Liza was bitterly disappointed, though apparently she was unaware of exactly why National General had suddenly backed out of the *Cuckoo* project. She had been ambitious in trying to get the role, but she had never pushed herself at the expense of other players. She knew her own ambitions and the ambitions of others and she recalled, without acrimony, when she had arrived for auditions and heard other actresses exclaim, 'Oh God, that's all we need. Judy Garland's daughter.' Liza was not about to take deliberate advantage of her name or rank.

She had not, in fact, been pushy in her career. She was simply always there, always ready. She had hounded—and haunted—producers by her mere presence, her shyness, her eagerness. But she was not prepared for selflessness on her behalf from others, certainly not from one like Alan Pakula who was not even a friend at this point. If she had known what was transpiring behind the scenes or what had happened, she might not have been able to cope with the situation, or, eventually, to play Pookie the way she did.

Despite the disappointment, she did keep herself busy. She was now a nightclub star and engagements were plentiful. She played the Talk of the Town in London in May of 1966, then the Cocoanut Grove in Los Angeles and thereafter a command performance before Prince Rainier and Princess Grace in Monaco.

It had been French singer-turned-actor Charles

Aznavour who had caught Liza's act at the Cocoanut Grove, been tremendously impressed by the girl on stage and off, and arranged for her concert at the Olympia Music Hall in Paris. The French, never partial to American performers, were on the whole ecstatic about Liza's stage appearance. One French newspaper announced, 'She doesn't interpret a song. She pulls it out of her heart.' Another Parisian paper compared her to the late Edith Piaf, 'The Sparrow', and lovingly referred to Liza as 'the American Piaf'. That was indeed a heady compliment.

Having been certified prime talent by the finicky French, Liza returned to the States to fulfil a summer tour of the musical *The Pajama Game*. This time there was no Lee Theodore (the choreographer of *Flora, the Red Menace*) to suddenly insist that Liza was no dancer and that her dancing interludes should be inexplicably cut from the show.

But despite all her professional activity, Liza was unsatisfied. There was the overriding dream of another Broadway show, or even better, a movie.

Ultimately, and unknown to Liza, it would be Mama who would come to the rescue by securing for her a cameo part in the British-made feature film, *Charlie Bubbles*.

CHAPTER TWELVE

Michael Medwin, the British actor who was producing *Charlie Bubbles* for Memorial Enterprises, was
a long-standing friend of Judy, and it was at her insti-
gation that Liza was auditioned for the small but
showy role of Eliza. The part called for the girl to
be an overly intellectual American would-be writer
who temporarily becomes the secretary and mistress
of successful writer Charlie Bubbles. Albert Finney,
the resourceful British actor who had gained such
acclaim for his celluloid delineation of *Tom Jones*, was
both to star in the title role and to direct the venture.

Liza was in Las Vegas when she received the call
from Finney, requesting that she audition in California. 'I didn't ask why,' Liza said. 'I figured if Albert
Finney wants to see you, you go.'

She auditioned a scene from Shelagh Delaney's
script with what Finney felt was too much intensity.
'Now read it like you really don't care,' he said. She
thought she had lost the role, but a few weeks later

Finney asked if she could be in London in two weeks to start filming.

Liza was tremendously impressed with the opportunity the film would afford her, but tried to be off-handedly casual in discussing the venture with the American press. 'The whole script,' she insisted, 'is kind of weird but it's good weird not crummy weird.'

Finney met a nervous Liza at London's Heathrow Airport. He was wearing a black zorro cape and plumed hat. 'He helped me into the rear of his chauffeured Rolls-Royce, then got in himself,' Liza recalls. 'After he shut the door, he took off his hat and cape and I saw he was wearing a lumberman's shirt and slacks. Then he opened the bar which he had stocked with beer and sandwiches.'

Liza may have been too eager to score in her first film. 'You have a face that registers everything,' Finney alerted her. 'It's not veiled enough. Do half of what you're doing.' It was advice that Liza would remember in playing future screen roles.

The filming of *Charlie Bubbles* was a pleasant, if brief experience for Liza, who was unaccustomed to the kind of gentleness that Finney possessed and displayed. 'All the time we were making the picture,' she later recalled with a touch of amazement, 'he never once lost his temper.'

Fourth-billed Liza actually had what amounted to a cameo in Charlie Bubbles. Established and experienced actress Billie Whitelaw, as Bubbles' ex-wife Lottie, was the dominant female spirit in the tale. But Liza did have one telling scene in this depressing tale of a writer who has sold out his integrity for capital gains and can find no reason for staying alive. In the course of the story, she accompanies Finney on a drive to Manchester to visit his young son (Timothy Garland). Liza and Finney spend the night together in a large hotel, where he passively allows the girl, who has shorn her wig, to make awkward love to him. Because of the short, off-camera sex act, the picture was tagged an 'adult' drama and in the United States was released by Universal's Regional Films. The most nudity one witnesses in this film is a hesitant Liza staring enraptured at Finney, she dressed only in her bra and panties (and his arms cover most of her from the waist down from the camera lens).

Producer Medwin thought that if he released the film first in the United States he might garner sufficient critical and audience interest to make the picture commercially more important in the British marketplace. *Charlie Bubbles* debuted in America in early 1968. It received some very favourable reviews—in fact it would be listed on some of the Ten Best Films of the Year Polls—but it was apathetically received by filmgoers in its art house release. The same situation occurred when it was released in England: good reviews but with little business. (During a mid-1974 reissue engagement in London, the film would fare much better.)

Liza's reviews for the film were mixed. Renata Adler, who spent a year in the dark reviewing for the *New York Times*, claimed Liza did her part '. . . wide-eyed and with her voice pitched to set the teeth on edge'. *Variety* was equally unimpressed: '. . . [she] gets a trifle cloying, but is okay'. The British, however, were far more appreciative of Liza's contributions to this bleak, English counterpart to America's *Young-blood Hawke*. Said the English *Monthly Film Bulletin*, '. . . [there is] a beautifully caricatured performance by Liza Minnelli as a cross between a slap-happy American in Europe and an eager student of "creative writing".' The British *Films and Filming* was even more laudatory of Judy's daughter: 'A superbly arranged set piece, it owes a great deal to the acting of Liza Minnelli.'

Charlie Bubbles actually left Liza's screen career in temporary limbo, since very few people in Hollywood would see the picture, or have the patience to sit through the introspective, highly intellectual sequences preceding Liza's short appearance on-camera.

Back in New York after *Charlie Bubbles*, Liza had ample time to put her personal life into order, or so she thought. She was enormously fond of Peter. She actually loved him in a way, and she owed him a great deal. It was Peter who encouraged her to have the 'forest of evil' that had been her waist-long hair cut into the boyish shag *à la* Mia Farrow. On Liza the hair style would never look fey nor, in turn, did it seem 'butch'. And it was Peter who supplied on a continuous basis that element of life that Liza had always felt was so important to life, namely, laughter or the illusion of laughter.

Having informed the press on several occasions that she and twenty-four-year-old Peter would soon wed, the couple actually appeared at New York's Municipal Hall on February 21st, 1967. Liza casually told the eager press, 'We've been engaged two years and it's taken us that long to get down here.'

The wedding, a small, private ceremony, took place on Friday, March 3rd, 1967, at the Manhattan apartment of Liza's most effective agent and very good friend, 'Stevie' (Stephanie) Phillips. Judge Joseph A. Macchia of the Civil Court performed the ceremony. Pamela Reinhardt, of Los Angeles, was the bridesmaid, with Paul Jasmen, of New York, as the best man. Later the small assemblage romped over to the Central Park West apartment of Liza's married business manager, Martin Bregman, for a lavish reception.

Liza was a radiant bride, but it was Judy, as usual, who stole the show. Arriving on the arm of Vincente Minnelli, the effervescent Garland then proceeded to become extremely chummy, affectionate even, with Sid Luft who, apparently, had made her life so miserable over the years and from whom she and her family needed the protection of detectives. Within months, Luft would again be managing Judy's career and, within a few months after that, there would again be the bitterness and hostility when Judy would feel that he had once more betrayed and cheated her by selling her contract with him as collateral for a monetary loan.

Coping with Judy would prove an awkward situation for the newlyweds. Judy was again in one of her 'down' periods and often Liza and Peter had to assume the responsibilities for the welfare of Lorna and Joey. 'Our house is a haven for them when Mama is in a bad mood and they need help and peace,' Liza wrote, apparently somewhat understating the case, in her *Good Housekeeping* magazine reminiscences in 1968.

Judy was at her most extreme in this period. Most of the time she refused to see Joey and Lorna. She had placed them in a separate wing of her hotel, with governesses, and would literally make a production out of her 'audiences' with them. She had become reclusive, ashamed of her dependence on drugs and ashamed of her brief participation in, and subsequent firing from, Twentieth Century-Fox's *Valley of the Dolls*, in which Susan Hayward replaced her.

The Jacqueline Susann novel-to-film project was one that Liza had warned Judy against from the beginning. 'They're using you, Mama. Don't do it,' Liza had said. She, more than anyone still alive, knew that at this stage of her life, Judy must not be exploited by anyone. It was Judy who must 'use' and exploit.

Liza immediately assumed the role of motherhood. 'Lorna, who's fifteen, has the *real* voice in the family, and we mean to help her in any way we can if she decides she wants a career. Joey is only twelve, and he needs a man around. Peter is that man.' Liza said it proudly and with sincerity.

Also during this period Liza was learning to insulate and protect herself from her mother. Realising that Judy's highs and lows were becoming even more extreme, her middles non-existent, and the damage that was accruing to Lorna, Joey and herself more pervasive, Liza simply shut herself, and the children, off from Judy and the more severe elements of the outside world.

'When she's in a low period,' Liza wrote, 'I don't answer the phone. Peter does. He takes care of all our mail and pays the bills and keeps me from going off the deep end over little things.'

Unfortunately, neither realised then that Peter was already playing the role of Mr Minnelli.

Judy eventually picked up some of the remnants of her career and the pieces of her life, and embarked on a concert tour which culminated in yet another Palace Theatre engagement in the summer of 1967. This time Lorna (vocalising) and Joey (on the drums) were used to bolster her strained act, and *this time* it would be Liza who repeatedly procrastinated about showing up to see her *alter ego* performing on stage. With Judy involved with her career again and being romanced by writer Tom Green (who did not become Mr Garland number five), and the children boarded with Nancy Barr, president of Liza's and Judy's fan clubs, Liza and Peter set out for their own concert tour, including Liza's first engagement in Australia where she appeared in a one-woman television special.

Chris and Peter became the opening bill in Liza's nightclub act, and the three made frequent appearances on *The Tonight Show Starring Johnny Carson.* The trio's careers were going well, but it was Liza who was beginning to emerge as a major attraction.

'I'm not a star—not yet,' she insisted. 'But I'm on my way. It's kind of an advantage [being Judy Garland's daughter]. I know why people come to see me. I hear them in the lobby talking. They expect a carbon copy or they expect me to be no good. Originality is one thing they don't expect.' Liza, as always, was full of zest and enthusiasm: 'Life could not possibly be boring ever. There is so much to see and do in the world.'

Her orbit into stardom was helped by her solo appearances on *The Kraft Music Hall* (the best being her sequence with Woody Allen), and on *The Carol Burnett Show* where Liza and Miss Burnett proved to be a deft comedy-singing team.

January of 1968 saw Liza opening triumphantly at the Empire Room of New York's Waldorf Astoria Hotel. The first-night crowd included such luminaries as Ethel Merman, Arlene Dahl, Hal Prince, Sheila MacRae, Ed Sullivan, Dionne Warwick, and Joel Grey. Liza's class act was greeted with proper enthusiasm, as was her striking outfit consisting of a thigh-high mini dress with short pink culottes underneath.

But there was trauma behind this potentially joyous occasion. Mama was in one of her now increasingly frequent periods of crisis. Judy had 'bombed' at Madison Square Garden in December, prematurely ending a scheduled week-long engagement, and on January 22nd, she lost the lead role in *Mame*, replacing Angela Lansbury on Broadway, to Janis Paige. Janis Paige! By Garland standards, the very talented Janis Paige was not even a star. Simultaneously, Judy, Lorna, and Joey were locked out of their Stanhope Hotel suite and their possessions confiscated for non-payment of bills.

Judy was 'down', all the way down, that evening of January 22nd, so Peter and Nancy Barr persuaded her to attend Liza's club performance. Judy was convinced that her career was at an end, so there was no further need now to be jealous of Liza on her way up while Mama was down and strictly out.

Liza graciously asked Judy to join her on stage. They duetted to *When the Saints Come Marching In*, then Judy offered a solo of the Gershwin song *Liza* with her elder daughter sitting worshipfully at her feet. The impact on the audience was overwhelming.

Another standing ovation, and all for Judy. She was 'up' again. Garland's whole lengthy career had been a succession of comebacks. Well, she would make yet another one. She was still the biggest star of them all.

First, however, she needed a place to live. She decided to ensconce herself, with Lorna and Joey, in Liza's Waldorf suite while Liza remained with Peter at her apartment on East 57th Street.

On Liza's closing night, January 27th, a once more proud and confident Mama threw a lavish party for her daughter in the Waldorf suite.

Liza, of course, got the bill.

CHAPTER THIRTEEN

In March, Liza received a call from Alan J. Pakula. He stated that he might have backing and distribution for *The Sterile Cuckoo*, and then asked her whether she could come to Los Angeles to test for Paramount executives.

She flew from Las Vegas on March 11, made the test, and then spent a few days with her father before leaving for Chicago and a concert at Roosevelt Auditorium.

The following months found Liza's career in high gear but also, professionally speaking, in a kind of limbo. She wanted *The Sterile Cuckoo* badly and was willing to sacrifice any opportunity to play the role upon which she had set her heart. Deliberately, she made only short-term commitments: appearances on *The Hollywood Palace*, the Grammy and Tony Award shows, and brief concert engagements.

By the time she left for Australia in June of 1968, to fill a three-week engagement at Chequers Club in Sydney, she still did not know whether she had the Pookie Adams role in *The Sterile Cuckoo*. It was during the Australian engagement that Liza met the country's Prime Minister, John Gorton, backstage. Supposedly, it was an innocuous encounter but in March, 1969, the incident became an international scandal. Liza and the Prime Minister were rumoured to have had an affair in Bali and Canberra, of all places, and Liza allegedly had 'told all' in an article for Britain's *Private Eye* magazine.

This 'scandal' was the beginning of Liza's image as a *femme fatale*, a titillating status that still persists. Although she made vehement denials of any romance, or even close association, with the Prime Minister, she also made a statement which, taken out of context, would add further flame to the mounting fire. 'He was really a very nice guy,' Liza said.

When the press caught up with Liza in Miami Beach, where she was rehearsing for her club engagement at the Deauville Hotel, she insisted that the romance rumours were 'vicious lies. . . . The entire story is untrue and ridiculous.' Liza glibly explained that she had even sent Gorton and his wife a telegram stating her intention of taking prompt legal action. 'I am going to sue whoever is causing trouble for the head of my husband's country.'

Meanwhile, despite the demands of Albert James, an Opposition party leader, to fifty-seven-year-old Gorton, the Australian House of Representatives voted not to delve into the charges that Gorton had behaved improperly, accepting instead his statement that he was just a victim of a cruel whisper campaign. Liza added in her remarks to the frenetic press, 'I've never written any article, I don't even have time to write letters. And I've never been in Bali in my life. . . .

Somebody is trying to pin some kind of rap on Gorton and his record is spotless.'

As Liza described the 'innocent' meeting after a Sydney nightclub performance that previous July, 'We were all a-flutter. It was like the President coming backstage. My mother-in-law and sister-in-law were there and we lined up in a sort of receiving line. He was really a very nice guy.

'I love Australia and can't believe the people would tolerate such a dishonest way of attacking someone. I cannot imagine that anyone would believe anything so absurd. I am appalled at such irresponsible statements that have no foundation in fact. They must be pretty desperate for a little scandal to use.'

If the media observed a certain respect when questioning Liza, no such tact was utilised when trying to reach Peter Allen for his reaction to the situation. One day he answered the hotel telephone to hear an announcer from a Sydney, Australia, radio station, 'You're on the air, Mr Allen. What do you think of the secret meetings between your wife and Mr Gorton?' According to Liza, Peter was so furious at this rude approach, he just screamed into the receiver.

Of course, by this time, it was widely rumoured that the marriage of Mr and Mrs Peter Allen was in trouble.

Nobody knows, or at least is willing to talk about, what happened to Liza's 'legal actions' against *Private Eye* and the other perpetrators of the story.

In Las Vegas, in July, 1968, Liza was about ready to accept the female lead in the Broadway musical, *Promises, Promises*, derived from the Billy Wilder film *The Apartment*, which had starred Shirley MacLaine.

It was to be the first stage musical by sensational hit-tune makers Burt Bacharach and Hal David and it seemed guaranteed a major success, particularly with David Merrick producing the heavily budgeted venture.

The role of Fran Kubelik from the 1960 film was one that practically every young and not-so-young star wanted. And Liza Minnelli, still, was considered by show biz professionals as a dark horse candidate for the role. Despite her Tony award, she was not a major box-office draw on the Great White Way at this time. The people who go to nightclubs and those who support the theatre, generally, are separate entities. For all these reasons, no one in her right mind in Liza's position would turn down such an opportunity.

However, Liza did. *The Sterile Cuckoo* was finally being offered to her.

Her decision was considered not only foolhardy but insane. Judy Garland's daughter, obviously, so the neon grapevine claimed, had inherited not only her mother's inability to guide her career wisely, but also an equal amount of that great star's self-destructiveness. After all, *The Sterile Cuckoo* might never be made and, if the plans for production actually materialised and the film was really completed, it probably would be a 'B' movie, the kind that might receive limited theatrical release but which more likely would find its major exposure on television. At the time the project was considered to be merely a whim of Pakula, a producer of proven ability who imagined himself a director. Paramount Pictures could indulge this whim if they could have options for his services on more important entertainment packages.

Moreover, Paramount objected to Liza Minnelli,

citing her poor track record in the recently released *Charlie Bubbles*. However, forty-year-old Pakula said, 'Liza was the only person I seriously considered for the role, despite pressure from the studio for a more established figure.' Even Alvin Sargent's original screenplay description of Pookie Adams sounded as if it had been written with Liza directly in mind. 'Sort of special to look at . . . wide eyes constantly searching and making mental notes . . . she's a lanky thing, put together with loose hardware that allows her to move in a way that most people haven't moved since they were kids.'

Production was set for September, 1968, with location filming at Hamilton College and Vernon Centre, New York, preceding studio work at Paramount's Hollywood studio. Liza would receive first billing (below the title) and a fee of $25,000.

How was Liza going to approach this weighty acting assignment? Would she rely on the teaching she had had years before at the Herbert Berghof classes in New York? Not really. As Liza would enjoy relating, '. . . my mother gave me my one great acting lesson. I was up for a TV show, *Ben Casey* or something, and the part was a pregnant girl who had an abortion that had gone wrong and she's in the hospital. I knew how I wanted to see it, but not how to be it. So I sort of gingerly took the script to Mama, and said, you know, "Mama, help me." We sat down on her floor, and she said, "Now, read me your lines, and the doctor's lines, both."

'His line was, "Did you want to have the baby?" I read it and Mama said, "All right, he's a doctor, he isn't getting personal—but how *dare* he intrude on you, how *dare* he ask you that, how *dare* he be there, how *dare* you be in the hospital, if only you could have married the father, if only he'd loved you, which he didn't. Now did you want to have the baby?"

'All I had to say was "No," but it came out right. Because she had given me the thoughts—the pause, not the line. Then she said, "Read me his line again," and I did, and she said, "Now this time you are going to concentrate on not crying. That's all you have to worry about, not letting him see you cry. Your baby is dead, your life is ruined, but you're not going to cry, you're a strong girl, your parents have told you, your teachers have told you, you *know* it, you *know* it, *you're not going to cry!*"

'And my "No" came out even better. She taught me how to—fill in the pauses. And if there is a way I act, that's the way. From that one day there on the floor.'

But now, when an excited Liza approached Mama to show her the script she received no professional or emotional support. Mama strongly disapproved of the film part. The character Liza was to play was weird and unsympathetic. Why would her 'Baby' want to play such a crummy role in a nothing movie when she could be starring on Broadway? Vincente, however, was excited by the screenplay and predicted that it would make Liza a major star.

Liza regarded Pookie Adams as '. . . a lost memory . . . someone everyone can identify with'. None the less, she thought of Pookie as a less than admirable character and, after viewing the completed film, Liza said, 'If I'd been more cautious I could have made her more appealing to the audience. But I like her too much. She improvises her life, and I sympathise.'

On the set, the star was living up to the Pookie Adams image. Local girls of high school and college age were recruited for the scenes filmed at Hamilton College and Liza found them almost as snobby as her one-time Scarsdale classmates.

'One was a minister's daughter,' Liza recalls, 'and she collected antiques and one was an artist and so forth and they finally asked about me. I told them my father was a pimp and all sorts of awful things!'

Pakula would later remember the making of *The Sterile Cuckoo* as one of the happiest times of his life . . . and it was largely because of Liza. 'I've never seen anybody get more joy out of working, and it's contagious,' he said in a *Newsweek* magazine interview in 1972. Liza has, he believes, a unique blend of instinct and intelligence. She was always punctual, always totally prepared and always eager to accept direction.

He remembered that she would sometimes come to him on the set and ask, 'Hey, boss, tell me the story again.'

'I'd tell her the story just as I'd tell it to a child, the most simplistic "Once upon a time" language, and that helped her. Something worked for her in that, something put her together.'

Yet Pakula found that he could work intellectually with her just as well as on an emotionally responsive level. 'I remember one scene where we had great difficulty,' he told *Newsweek*. 'I was trying to explain what I wanted and I talked a lot, possibly more than I should have. After a while she got up and said, "OK, let's try it." She did, and it was right.'

Pakula was amazed and asked what he had said that had made her so completely responsive to his ideas. 'It was nothing you said,' Liza confided to him, 'I just watched your eyes and realised that unconsciously in your eyes you were really doing what you wanted me to, but you couldn't express it.'

Two sequences in the film were especially memorable and would be instrumental in earning Liza her first Academy Award nomination. In the first, a warmheartedly comic seduction sequence between the eager Pookie and the shy Jerry, the rapport was readily apparent between Liza and her co-star, Wendell Burton, the unknown recruited from the San Francisco stage production of *You're a Good Man, Charlie Brown.*

The scene was shot in a seedy motel at Sylvan Beach, a declining resort community on Lake Oneida in upstate New York. It was October and the chill winds from the lake and the shoddiness of the surroundings somehow enabled Liza and Burton to set the screen aglow with their largely improvised enactment of an experience, the loss of innocence, that comes to almost everyone.

The second treasured scene in *The Sterile Cuckoo* was Pookie's climactic five-minute-long telephone monologue in which she suddenly realises that the special romance between herself and Jerry is at an end. The virtual non-stop, one-woman scene inside a cramped dormitory telephone booth would have posed an enormous challenge to even the most experienced of actresses, and it would ensure Liza her first Academy Award nomination.

'We had yakked it out in rehearsal,' Liza remembered, 'but I didn't know how to work it. I was scared to death—but right before I stepped in front of a camera it hit me like a rock, and I just did it.'

The scene, which ranks with Luise Rainer's famous telephone moment in *The Great Ziegfeld*, was shot in one take. 'I couldn't believe that would happen,' Pakula said, 'but it did, and the best part is that blank, numb face of her at the end which is absolutely dead right.'

Liza called that bit '. . . "her willy"—like for the first time she doesn't know what to do at all.' It was a feeling that Liza had experienced before.

Exactly one year later, however, Liza would regard as impertinent questions from *Life* magazine's Thomas Thompson on exactly how she had played the crucial telephone sequence. She was particularly tender and vulnerable when he continued probing just what emotions and experiences she had drawn upon for her celluloid histrionics.

Typically, she disguised her hostility, and most likely, her tinge of resentment for the moment. The next day she encountered Thompson and told him that he had given her 'trouble' the night before.

'You started me thinking that people are going to look at that telephone scene and they're going to say, 'Poor girl, she's acting out her own life." That girl isn't me,' Liza insisted. 'My parents didn't play this scene. Hollywood didn't play this scene. I played this scene! Me! My ability played this scene!'

Her anger was obviously mounting and there was no protective publicist present to cover Liza's emotional tracks, when she proclaimed, 'I've plotted my life *step* by *step*. *I* didn't just happen! When are people going to stop making comparisons?'

Finally reaching what is, for an actress, the point of fever pitch, Liza characteristically drew back and let out the low, familiar wail that would become her perennial lament.

'When can I be me?'

CHAPTER FOURTEEN

Soon she would have the chance to become herself, but there were doors she wanted to leave unopened and the opportunity would be rejected in favour of contriving the public image of what Liza, at this time, decided the *real* Liza should be.

She concluded 1968 professionally with a guest starring appearance on the ABC-TV musical series, *That's Life* starring Robert Morse and E. J. Peaker. As an office worker in the December 17th instalment, Liza sang *A Secretary Is Not a Toy* from Morse's Broadway success, *How to Succeed in Business without Really Trying*. Liza's presence on the show did nothing to help improve the ratings of the abortive programme.

The next year, 1969, would be a difficult one for Liza. It would have its tragedies and its triumphs and it would be the most important year of young Liza's life. Her mother would die, her marriage would begin its final collapse, and Liza would emerge a distinctive international star. It would also be the year in which

n the town in New York with Desi Arnaz, Jnr
ebruary, 1973).

With 'fiancé' Desi Arnaz, Jnr, on the set of
Marco in Tokyo in July, 1972.

ith Peter Sellers at Shepperton Studios in London (May, 1973).

The Winter Garden Theatre engagement (January, 1974).

With businessman David J. Mahoney, fashion designer Halston, and actress Marisa Berenson at Maxim's in Paris (November, 1973).

With Alice Cooper in 1973.

With Lorna Luft at the Rainbow Room party following the Winter
Garden Theatre opening (January 6, 1974).

With Vincente Minnelli at the Rainbow Room party.

Onstage at the Winter Garden Theatre.

Backstage at the Winter Garden
Theatre (January, 1974).

With Jack Haley, Jnr, on the MGM backlot for *That's Entertainment*
(1974).

ith husband Jack Haley, Jnr, on their wedding
y—September 15, 1974.

Liza today.

Liza would reject her new, honestly acquired image and, instead, perpetuate the impression of herself as Sally Bowles, the character she was still determined to play sometime, somewhere. Liza knew that a film version of *Cabaret* was being planned and she knew she would have the support of composers Fred Ebb and John Kander when it came time to cast the lead role for this screen musical.

Meanwhile, life was hectic for Liza. She was in Paris in January, flew to Puerto Rico in February to fulfil a nightclub engagement, and then returned to France to tape a European television special. The month of March found her in Paris, Los Angeles, New York, and Miami.

It was in Puerto Rico, outside the Ocho Club in San Juan, that Liza found a maimed wild dog that had just been castrated in a canine fight. She fed the poor beast chopped meat but did not immediately take it as her own. However, the mutt decided that he would adopt Liza, and by the time she left Puerto Rico the animal would be 'family', living grandly on a diet of steak and caviar. When Papa Minnelli first encountered the bedraggled animal, now named Ocho, he commented, 'That's the best imitation of a dog I ever saw.'

Not everyone would agree. The dog was unfriendly and many considered the four-legged creature to be vicious. Afraid of most people, he sometimes snapped at strangers and one such person, a wardrobe attendant in Miami, would claim that Ocho's 'death grip' on her hand had caused such severe injuries that she had lost partial use of it, though at the time there was no bleeding and she had refused medical attention. In court, the woman collected seven and a half thousand dollars for alleged medical expenses incurred months after the incident. By this time, the elderly Ocho had been de-fanged and was subsisting royally and heathily on the richest of foods. 'Diseased gums,' explained the defiant Liza in court, insisting that that, and not his alleged viciousness, had been the reason for the extraction.

In early April, Liza signed with Otto Preminger to play the leading role in *Tell Me That You Love Me, Junie Moon* which was to begin production in June. 'Autocratic Otto' had seen work prints of *The Sterile Cuckoo* at Paramount where he was preparing to cast *Junie Moon*. Immediately he became convinced that Liza was about to become a major motion picture star. Best of all, he craftily perceived that few directors or producers were aware yet of her budding screen magic and he could probably sign her to a long-term contract at a very cheap price. (Jill Haworth, who had played Sally Bowles in the Broadway *Cabaret*, had been one of his cinema 'discoveries'.)

Liza and her agent, however, demanded fifty thousand dollars and a strictly one-picture deal. Preminger, who was renowned for his dogmatic stands, protested that the sum mentioned was too much money, and, regardless of whatever price they agreed upon, he insisted on' options for future pictures with Liza. Liza and her representatives said, 'Nein.'

'Tell Miss Minnelli,' Preminger bellowed at her agent, Stevie Phillips, 'that there are many brilliant young actresses dying to play this part. Ask her what she thinks of that!'

Liza, replying through her intermediaries, said that she was happy for Mr Preminger who had all those other actresses to choose from but, personally, she would rather throw up than commit herself to future productions with him. Preminger was livid, but Liza won her one-picture deal—and the fifty thousand dollars.

Tell Me That You Love Me, Junie Moon, from the acclaimed novel by Marjorie Kellogg, was the sensitive story of three physically and emotionally handicapped people who, oppressed by hospital life, secure their release and attempt to make their way together in a sometimes hostile world. Liza played Junie Moon, a girl horribly disfigured by acid thrown in her face by a disgruntled lover.

By June 10th, having completed her Las Vegas engagement at the Sahara Hotel, Liza was ready for the *Junie Moon* rehearsals. She had thoroughly immersed herself in the role. She had been to hospitals to examine photographs of disfigured women and also to observe the behaviour of such women when confronted by strangers, the manner in which they might attempt to hide their deformities or, in some cases, to flaunt them.

Junie Moon, as depicted by Miss Kellogg in her novel and in her screenplay, was a withdrawn, reserved woman of extraordinary courage and fortitude, a creature seemingly with little emotion who was screaming with frustration on the inside. It was a role, if not a film, that would serve Liza well in the months ahead.

On June 22nd, 1969, Judy Garland was dead.

Considering the demands of the crisis, Liza behaved admirably throughout the aftermath of her mother's tragic end. But there were many whose enmity she had unknowingly provoked who were quick to say that her mother's funeral was providing Liza with the role of a lifetime in a spectacle that could never be topped. They seemed to delight in concocting the wildest interpretations for her every action.

The unexpected depth and sensitivity of Liza's statements to the press were given as evidence of her role-playing in a script that many believed to have been ghosted by the ever-present and multi-talented Kay Thompson, who had been such a strong influence on Garland years before at Metro. Then, the fact that Liza was photographed wearing dark glasses after selecting her mother's coffin was offered as complete proof that Liza was so dependent on drugs that she had indeed lost touch with reality. The harsh glare of sunlight, they said, would send her freaking into madness.

Not only was Liza's behaviour in this time of extreme stress subjected to absurd criticism, the past was even more inanely analysed. If her detractors were to have their way, Liza's budding career would be buried with her mother. It did not happen that way at all, of course, but her enemies were correct in one regard: Liza's past was being entombed with Judy Garland. Her decades-long Cinderella nightmare as Judy's gangling, awkward daughter was coming to an end. Ahead lay a life that would be rich and full . . . perhaps too rich and too full. If Judy Garland had lived eighty lives in one, Liza could reach for a hundred and eighty. But there would be a substantial difference in the way the lives would be played out.

Upon being told once never to forget the rainbow,

Judy is said to have retorted, 'Rainbow, rainbow . . . how can I forget the rainbow? I've had rainbows up my ass.' Liza, on the other hand, would carry the rainbow over her shoulder and she would know who she was and where she was going every step of the way.

The funeral now a thing of the past, Liza turned her full attention to *Junie Moon*. The movie itself would prove a disaster for everyone concerned, except Liza and her talented co-stars: Ken Howard, Robert Moore, and James Coco. The film would receive only limited theatrical release and, at the time, many in the motion picture community predicted that its failure, earning less than one million dollars in North American distributors' rentals, and coming immediately after the equally poor *Skidoo*, would end the sixty-four-year-old Preminger's lengthy film career. It almost did. However, there was *Such Good Friends* with Dyan Cannon and the director returned to the medium again in late 1974 with a new project, *Rosebud*, starring Peter O'Toole.

The making of *Junie Moon* was a nightmare for everyone. Preminger, apparently, was determined to demonstrate with *Junie Moon* that he was as 'hip' and 'with it', fashionable phrases of the time, as when he had made *Laura* (1944), *The Moon Is Blue* (1953), and *The Man with the Golden Arm* (1955). For this purpose he surrounded himself with a small battalion of young film-makers and would-be film-makers. The idea was to have these 'promising' youths compete for prizes, never publicly announced, by making movies on the making of a major movie.

The smell of marijuana hung over the location sets,

sometimes as strong as disinfectant in a lavatory. Because of the nature of the plot and the hippie fashions of the time, the production generally gave the impression of Herr Otto attempting a freak show variation on the Marx Brothers state-room sequence in *A Night at the Opera*.

However, Preminger did not stint on technical talent. He had Boris Kaufman, the pioneering cameraman of the early 1930s (*L'Atalante*, *Zero de Conduite*), setting up shots, and Lyle Wheeler (who later had his name removed from the film's credits) as the talented production designer. (He had done the art direction on such landmark movies as *Gone with the Wind* and *Rebecca*.) On the Massachusetts sets, Preminger's odd group of protégés convinced themselves that this new project would prove how antediluvian were such trend-setting 1960s films as *Medium Cool*, *Faces*, and *Last Summer*.

The student film-makers on the set had increased from a planned five to an unspecified mob, and no one seemed to have an exact count of how many contestants were present. They seemed to be everywhere, filming nearly everything and everyone in sight with an abandon that verged on the slapstick. Preminger was trying to be their god, their idol, and he played the role to the hilt. When things were going well, as happened on occasion, when the more than competent performers were able to display their too little utilised talents, the famed director would cross his hands as if in supplication and assume a yoga-like position. He would be like a baby Buddha now, unmoving and serene as the student film-makers gathered worshipfully at his side.

Liza had more than her share of problems during the making of this film. At the Salem, Massachusetts, location site, she was rather testy with the press, exclaiming, 'My private life is nobody's business.' Then, as if to apologise to the news force, she explained, 'Besides I lead a very routine, normal, boring life. Why should anybody be interested? When people get curious I try not to be rude but to head them off at the pass.'

More serious trouble brewed when the company moved to the Quincy, Massachusetts, filming locations.

In nearly every Otto Preminger production of recent decades there is at least one facet of the filming that receives extraordinary attention from the press. This time it happened because of a shooting episode at the Blue Hills graveyard.

The scenario demanded that Junie Moon accompany her peculiar—it turns out he is psychotic—date (Ben Piazza) to the local cemetery where he asks her to strip naked. She consents and while disrobing he begins mumbling obscenities in order to get sexually aroused. Liza's Junie Moon then makes the mistake of laughing at his stream-of-consciousness fetish and he in turn beats her and then casually pours car battery acid on her face and arm.

However, there was an 1880s Massachusetts statute still on the books which declared that anyone who creates a nuisance in a graveyard is guilty of a misdemeanour and subject to a fine ranging from one to one hundred dollars. A woman, whose husband was buried in the cemetery, brought a cause of action against Preminger and company, and the press had a field day. At the cost of a one-hundred-dollar fine it was perhaps the least expensive publicity Preminger ever achieved. And of course much was made of the fact that *the* daughter of the recently late Judy Garland, who *should* have been in mourning, was instead involved in some too adult film-making in a cemetery.

Then, when the *Junie Moon* cast and crew moved to Naples, Florida, in early September, 1969, they encountered further difficulties with the International Alliance of Theatrical Stage Employees' local organisation, which was insistent that Preminger indulge in some expansion of his existing camera crew. In anger, Preminger whisked his company back to Hollywood. Once there, and shooting at Paramount, production had to be temporarily halted one day when Liza suddenly suffered from a kidney stone attack. It was Preminger who had Liza conveyed to the hospital and waited six hours while she was responding to treatment.

Liza would not be the first performer to discover belatedly that working on an Otto Preminger film could be an artistically unrewarding experience. It may have been a wise antidote against deep depression at Mama's death, but the rapport that she had enjoyed with her director during *The Sterile Cuckoo* was missing with Preminger. The latter, a director of the old authoritarian Erich von Stroheim school, preferred his actors on the set to be animated puppets rather than thinking human beings. Interestingly, just as Liza and her managers had won the financial battle regarding the *Junie Moon* contract, so Liza won the artistic contest on the set. Preminger left Liza pretty much to herself, somewhat surprisingly, out of consideration for her emotional strain over Judy's death, but largely because of his awe of this self-contained, new-generation actress. Kay Thompson (who had served a similar function for Judy back in the MGM days) served as an intermediary between the star and director on more than one occasion.

If Liza seemed in a daze to some on-the-set observers, it was more her way of digging into her off-beat screen role. She was fully aware of Mr Preminger's presence, his methods, and his unfulfilled hopes in moulding her performance to his assembly-line demands. She would later recount, '. . . Otto's theory is that the actor is hired to act, and he must be ready at all times. He wants the work done immediately, and perfectly. You get the impression with Otto that you don't have time to ask questions, and you come in and don't ask, and if you do it wrong, you get yelled at. It's like teachers. There are some who correct you by saying, "It would be better this way," and others who just say, "*That's wrong!*" And Otto is, um, the latter.'

Liza also took time to tell the press how she prepared for the traumatic sequence in *Junie Moon* in which she must see just how disfigured her face has become. 'Of course I got used to how it looked, so before the scene where I have to stare in the mirror and cry with shock, I went into a room by myself and told myself every ghost story I could think of, scared the bejesus out of myself—funny way to make a living, isn't it?'

Much later, *Newsday* newspaper critic Joseph Gelmis would ask Liza just what she had learned from Preminger. 'Never to make another movie with him,' she replied.

And the reviewers bore out her contention. Perhaps

Lloyd Ibert's review in the *Independent Film Journal* best summed up the faulted results of the Minnelli–Preminger on-camera alliance: 'Liza Minnelli, who, if she plays her career cards right, will become one of the great actresses of the seventies, is never given any opportunity to build a characterisation with all those wham-bam scenes flying by. But her agonised cry when she discovers her lover has died in her arms suggests what *Junie Moon* as a film should have achieved.'

When *Junie Moon* was to be distributed in England, the British film censor John Trevelyan demanded that the scene in which Liza writhes on the ground after having acid spilt in her face must be deleted.

'You are a butcher!' Otto is said to have protested. 'And you—you are a sadist!' Trevelyan concluded.

Junie Moon did make a brief appearance at the Cannes Film Festival in 1970. Ironically, while it received little attention, another American entry did. It was *M*A*S*H* produced by Otto's brother Ingo.

The final word on *Junie Moon* seems to have been uttered by the critic who rhetorically asked, 'Tell Me Why You Do It, Otto Preminger [certainly a more appropriate title for the director's distortion of the Kellogg novel-scenario],' and then added, 'His record for debasing the popular to the vulgar is unblemished.'

CHAPTER FIFTEEN

'Life is a cabaret, old chum,' sang Liza Minnelli in the show-stopping finale of her sensational appearance at the Olympia in Paris in December, 1969.

Her marriage to Peter seemed beyond repair. Her success by now had far eclipsed his, the opening of *The Sterile Cuckoo* having made her a major motion picture star who was being offered two hundred and fifty thousand dollars per film. In turn, this new status sent her nightclub and concert career skyrocketing.

Liza was now a superstar—nascent or full-blown—and her husband was still a small-time performer living uneasily in her shadow. 'We were playing *A Star Is Born* together,' explained Liza. The marital union just did not, could not work. No way. There seemed no alternative but still Liza did not seek a divorce. Was she perhaps hanging back out of gratitude for the past, or in a vain hope that something might just possibly work out, or purely because Peter represented some form of stability way back in her life?

Throughout all of this, Liza was emotionally on her own. And she was living the life style of Sally Bowles to the hilt. She was making it apparent that the producers could not conceivably cast anybody else in the role for the motion picture version of *Cabaret*. The public simply would not permit it.

Liza was Sally. Sally was Liza.

Cabaret literally became Liza's theme song. It was her special property. 'In English you say "terrific". In French, you lack for words,' wrote one Parisian of her latest performance at the Olympia, in which Liza demonstrated that she was very much her Mama's child. During the course of one song, whose English lyrics seem to have escaped the Gallic audience, Liza 'forgot' the words and in the best Judy-sympathy tradition, ad-libbed a fumbled cover-up before sailing into a hearty finale.

Offstage, one needed a huge scorecard to keep count of Liza's enthusiastic romances. There was French singer-composer-actor and matinée idol Charles Aznavour who described his relationship with Liza as 'better than romance'. There was jet-set playboy Baron Alexis de Rede (he even named a racehorse after her). There was Jean Pierre Cassel, and later, Jean Claude Brially, two of France's most romantic cinema stars. And then there would be Rex Kramer (once Kulbeth) from Smackover, Arkansas, who would propel Liza into the ranks of international *femmes fatales*.

It was perfect and Peter, bless him, knew just how to handle the situation: 'Rex was exactly opposite from me; he was a country boy who hated the city and loved girls,' Peter told *Time* magazine. Speaking of Liza's decidedly unpredictable and unexpected relationships, Allen noted that '. . . she tends to react from one situation to another'.

With Rex Kramer, it looked as if Liza were going back to her roots. She began 'seriously' talking about spending the rest of her life on a farm in Arkansas eating black-eyed peas and grits.

Incredibly, some gullible people actually took Liza's fantasies of the simple life seriously. This group of naïve people did not include Peter Allen, who knew the many layers of Liza's personality pretty well by now. 'I knew she hadn't really gone country when she also mentioned that Ocho still ate only steak and caviar,' he said.

Meanwhile, Liza's career was continuing to soar upward. She had been announced to co-star with Academy Award winner Estelle Parsons in *I Never Promised You a Rose Garden* (a project that would be cancelled), NBC wanted her for a television special and, best of all, she had been nominated for an Academy Award as Best Actress of 1969 for her performance in *The Sterile Cuckoo*. (The picture would eventually gross in excess of 6·4 million dollars in United States and Canadian rentals alone.) It was one of those rare seasons in which outstanding female performances dominated the screen, and her competition was unusually tough: Genevieve Bujold (*Anne of the Thousand Days*), Jane Fonda (*They Shoot Horses, Don't They?*) Jean Simmons (*The Happy Ending*) and Maggie Smith (*The Prime of Miss Jean Brodie*).

A few weeks before the Oscar ceremonies Liza decided to try the Ann-Margret bit, zooming through Los Angeles on a motorcycle, a vehicle on which she had little experience and of which she had little knowledge. 'Now my word for motorcycles is "Hello, Death," '

Liza said after she suffered a serious fall from the speeding conveyance. (One version of the story had it that she had been dining with actor Tony Bill, and then, upon leaving the restaurant, she had decided to have a ride on his cycle.) It is known that the cycle hit an oil slick on Sunset Boulevard, and as Liza recalls, 'The next thing I knew a big light was shining in my face and a policeman was saying, "You're going to be all right." '

All right proved to be a relative matter. Her shoulder was fractured, twenty-nine stitches were required for her face, a front tooth was broken, and she suffered kidney damage. Hospitalised in serious, if not critical, condition, Liza is said to have amazed doctors when, after five days, she insisted on leaving the hospital.

'I just couldn't be bothered to stay in bed any longer,' she explained. Besides, she did not want to attend the Academy Awards looking like Junie Moon and she had to find some way to make her scratches and scarred face presentable. Charlie Schram, Liza's make-up man on *Junie Moon*, came to the rescue by applying the layers of magical Hollywood cosmetics that would disguise the scars and scratches on her battered face. 'I may have looked all right, but I was in a daze,' Liza said afterwards of that April 7th, 1970, when she attended the Awards at the Dorothy Chandler Pavilion on the arm of a proud, but nervous, Vincente.

'The doctor had given me something,' Liza recalls. 'He said it was just a mild pain-killer. But I never take pills—even one aspirin knocks me out. So I sat there not knowing what was going on.'

When Maggie Smith was announced as Best Actress, Liza is supposed to have applauded loudly and yelled, 'Wonderful . . . she's great,' without immediately realising that she herself had just lost the award.

At the official party following the Oscar ceremonies, a dopily freaked-out Liza determined to obtain for herself a permanent souvenir of the evening. Coyly pretending to have something in her eye, she asked her long-time idol Fred Astaire if she could borrow his handkerchief and then quickly pocketed the prize trophy. 'It has his initials on it,' she later boasted.

The day after the Oscar telecast, Liza had a special public announcement of her own. She and Peter Allen were separating. Although it could not have come as much of a surprise to Peter, he registered shock and disbelief to reporters, insisting it must have been caused by Liza's reaction to listening to false friends who predicted that Peter would be terribly jealous if she won an Academy Award.

'What a crazy thing to say,' Peter voiced. 'But Liza must have gone to the awards with some seeds of doubt in her mind that I might object to her winning an Oscar. Those are the kind of people who put all the pressure on us.'

Later Allen would amend his position to say, 'We separated so that we will have something to put back together again—not to get a divorce. . . . I love Liza, and Liza and I are the only two people who have to know it or believe it.'

Back in Hollywood, Liza would insist that the break-up '. . . was just due to the pressures of trying to be a super-everything. It had nothing to do with the Oscar nor with the motorcycle accident.'

By May, when Liza attended the Cannes Film Festival, it was common knowledge that the lead in the movie *Cabaret* would be hers. Filming was scheduled to start before the end of the year in Germany with stage choreographer-director Bob Fosse, who had directed the movie of *Sweet Charity* (1970), now set to direct the big new musical.

Liza's first American television special was telecast by NBC on June 29th, its airing in the summer doldrums of programming suggesting that the network was as unhappy with the show as Liza. She had wanted a one-woman programme. The network insisted on so-called 'guest stars' and somehow all had agreed on the bizarre combination of Anthony Newley, Michael J. Pollard, Randy Newman, and a host of even lesser-knowns. It was the sort of variety outing that could be considered a 'special' only in the midst of the glut of summer re-runs. Nevertheless, the programme turned out to be modestly respectable, the ratings were passable, and the event was moderately enjoyable. But it was still routine: Ron Field's choreography did not properly showcase Liza, the premise of a tribute to show business just did not come off, and Liza somehow could not shoulder the burden of enlivening the programme.

The early 1970s were a time of turmoil in America and the world and it was fashionable for performers, who only wanted to attract publicity, to crusade for the causes in which they supposedly believed. Not Liza!

Vernon Scott of the United Press International News Service complained—with tongue in cheek—in June, 1970, that Liza was not behaving 'normally' for a young superstar. 'She has missed out on mass rock festivals, has borne no babies out of wedlock, refused to picket or invade military installations and does not live on Indian reservations to demonstrate her empathy,' Scott wrote.

'I've suffered enough in my life,' Liza explained. 'I was raised with so much drama I don't crave it,' she added. 'I'm an observer and like to draw a line between what is fantasy and what is not.

'I feel I'm part of the "now" generation but,' Liza qualified, 'watching it—it's like I watched the '50s in Hollywood when I was a child. I like everything I see because I know it will go away,' she added.

One thing that would not go away, however, was her continuing obsession with *Cabaret*. She knew that the Broadway production, successful though it and the many road show versions had been, fell short of achieving the potential dramatic force that was inherent in the show. Above all, she sensed that the weakness lay largely in the projected characterisation of Sally Bowles.

She immersed herself totally into the 1930s, studying the caricatures of George Crosz, the films of Elisabeth Bergner, and the music of Kurt Weill. She got the 'look' of Sally from Louise Brooks, a near-legendary American actress who had appeared in German films in the late 1920s and early 1930s, and from another exotic cinema figure of the times, Lya du Putti. And Liza rejected, in totality, the costumes designed for her by Charlotte Fleming. They did not

139

seem true to the period, according to Liza, and eventually she and Broadway star Gwen Verdon, then Fosse's wife, accumulated the entire wardrobe by rummaging through old thrift shops and buying used outfits.

Cabaret, on film, was to depart considerably from the stage version, and the character of Sally would be strengthened. Still, Liza was having difficulty trying to 'find' the specific way to play Sally. 'She just looks like a kook and a kook gets boring unless she's specific,' Liza told Craig Zadan several months before the picture actually began production.

The Sally Bowles of *Cabaret* was a professional eccentric, an American girl who went to Germany as an actress, cultivated a bizarre, decadent image, and became a small-time cabaret singer and layabout. In the course of the story she has an abortion after a brief affair with a bisexual who had offered to marry her.

As the months passed and the start of filming was postponed until early 1971, Liza found the key to Sally's character. She realised that she did know Sally, that she had known many Sallys. 'I don't find Sally admirable, but I do find her understandable,' she admitted.

'Sally is a girl who improvises her whole life,' Liza declared, 'and her fantasy of tomorrow is so strong that she really can't take a good look at now.'

Meanwhile, the real-life Liza Minnelli had to take a good look at the present. Following the mild disaster of her television special came the release in July of *Tell Me That You Love Me, Junie Moon*. The picture attracted less public attention than had the cemetery nude scene and Preminger's court case.

The commercial apathy to *Junie Moon* wounded Liza, but she was comforted by the fact that it had not been her interpretation of the picture's concept which had wreaked havoc with the original novel. What did hurt was the judgment of such critics as Paul D. Zimmerman of *Newsweek* magazine. He seemed to be summing up the professional consensus when he complained that Liza '. . . risks becoming nothing more than a copy of herself repeated endlessly, film after film.'

'How many times', Zimmerman asked, 'will the public want to see Pookie Adams.'

Liza seemed very much aware of the neurotic screen image ('I've been hurt') that she had created, and she was now determined to break this present mould, both on screen and off. She wanted the world at large to know and understand that she was a free-spirited, fun-loving, exuberant gal who was living life for every pleasure it was worth without, however, the obvious use of drugs or pills. For Liza, the magical turn-on, it seemed, was sheer energy, the rapport she could create with an audience, plus surrounding herself with people who could make her laugh loud and continuously.

Still, there were problems in Liza's private life The 'magic' was going from her romance with drummer-guitarist Rex Kramer, and her father was seriously ill.

Vincente, however, was able to attend Liza's club opening at the Now Grove of the Los Angeles Ambassador Hotel in June, 1970, where she achieved a standing ovation. At the party afterwards, Gayle Martin, Liza's close friend, arrived on the arm of seventeen-year-old Desi Arnaz, Jnr, who, the hostess noted, had really grown up. Indeed he had, and he made Rex Kramer, several years Desi's senior, seem a mere guppy.

Liza's ideas and life-style, though hardly differing from the past, began to mirror the *Cabaret* philosophy, at least in regard to her love life. She continued her affair with Rex, resumed relations with Peter and remained, as she loosely put it, 'joined at the hip', to Fred Ebb.

Filming on *Cabaret* finally began in Munich in February, 1971. Vincente had just undergone surgery in Los Angeles and Liza was worried about him, but his recuperation seemed to be progressing well.

Liza tried to immerse herself totally in the film-making. She wanted to know as much as she could about the times, the decadence of Germany in the early 1930s, but everywhere she went she found hostility and resentment.

'I mean, you can't even find anyone who will admit he's a German,' Liza explained with a shriek. 'They're all Austrians.'

None the less, she found evidences of the past and evidence that the past really was not as dead as the natives were claiming. In Munich, she and Rex found an apartment in the *Schwabing*, a Bohemian neighbourhood where, as Liza phrased it, '. . . there were swastikas on the walls and riots going on.' In Bavaria, there were similar facets of life, and in Hamburg she found remnants of the kind of perverseness which *Cabaret* tried so diligently to depict: lesbians groping on stage and in mud puddles, live pornographic sex shows in which members of the audience were invited to participate, and sexual kinkiness galore.

The filming of *Cabaret* was a stimulating challenge and a pleasure for Liza. She got along well with her co-stars Joel Grey, recreating his stellar Broadway role, Michael York, Helmut Griem, and Marisa Berenson. And she had a marvellous rapport with Fosse and Gwen. It was nearly six months of exhaustive torturous work, but it was all coming together in a final product which Liza thought would be something special. She was very happy.

There was only one problem—Rex Kramer. Rex was one of Liza's back-up musicians in groups variously known as The Bojangles, The Wire Band, and Fred's Wire Band, and it was he who had guided Liza from the standard musical repertoire into more contemporary rock songs. But Rex, like Liza, was married and his wife (Margaret Louise) was pressing suit against Liza for alienation of affection. In her 556,000-dollar case, Margaret Louise claimed that Liza '. . . by use of great power, wealth, and influence, gained the affection of Rex Kramer and enticed him to abandon his wife'. Liza responded that she had not been 'the pursuer in this matter'. The case was eventually settled out of court, but Liza apparently suspected there had been some degree of conspiracy. Thereafter she felt that she had been 'used'.

Hurt, disappointed, and bored with it all, she tried to break off the relationship, but unless there was another man in her life, Rex would remain at her side.

At that time Liza was working twelve to sixteen hours each day on *Cabaret* and she was virtually near the point of physical collapse, 'an el foldo' as she called it. Taking on a new lover at this point was the height of absurdity to her. None the less, with the aid of her ever loyal secretary-companion Deanna Wenble, Liza managed to convince Rex that there was, indeed, a new man in her life. Exit Rex Kramer!

Afterwards, Liza (or maybe Deanna Wenble) could not resist boasting of the deception. Kramer is one of the few people who has unkind words to say about her. According to Rex, Liza is a psychological and emotional mess on constant ups and downs, dependent like Mama on aids to put her in the mood for any type of living.

No one paid very much credence to Kramer's assorted stories until the spring of 1974 when Liza's contradictory public statements about marriage and retirement and her continually 'spaced out', bleary-eyed appearance reminded many on-the-spot observers of drug-induced myopia. 'Wafting, just wafting,' say Liza's friends. Time, perhaps, will tell.

CHAPTER SIXTEEN

The summer of 1971 found Liza the darling of the jet set, her now close friend Marisa Berenson of *Cabaret* having provided the needed introductions. The divine Liza was now being linked, publicly and privately, with the Baron Alexis de Rede, whom she had known for some time.

In September, however, Liza fulfilled an engagement at the Greek Theatre in Los Angeles. Re-enter Desi Arnaz, Jnr, who followed her to engagements in Las Vegas and Lake Tahoe, to set the fires for an on-again-off-again romance that would make the twosome, but most especially Liza, the rage of the fan magazines, gossip papers, and news weeklies for the coming years.

Desi, seven years younger than Liza and already the sheik of Hollywood, had been accused at his tender age of the seduction and abandonment of ageing Hollywood juvenile and Oscar winner Patty 'The Miracle Worker' Duke. At age twenty-five, she was now claiming that her infant son, Sean, was the climax of her affair with Desi. Patty was married at the time, but this was Hollywood, where marital contracts have been known to have little connection with family life. Patty was absolutely certain that pubescent Desi had been the father of her child.

'She used him,' said Desi's mother, the perennially phenomenal Lucille Ball.

Desi did not feel 'used'. He felt proud as a rooster. He visited the infant the day after the birth and reported, 'It was an incredible sensation. He looks just like me.'

But marriage, then, was not a part of Desi's plans, at least not with Patty, who eventually got a divorce from her estranged husband of nineteen days, record producer Mike Tell, and then later married actor John Astin.

With Liza, however, Desi proposed right away, though it has never been absolutely clear just what he actually proposed. They exchanged rings, wedding bands, but Liza was still officially betrothed to Peter Allen and Desi (still under the protective wing of mother Lucy) was not eager for marriage. Neither was Liza.

Lucille Ball, however, was overwhelmed with expectation and happiness. Lucy had to be surrounded by winners and, as yet, neither Desi, Jnr, nor young Luci had shown the requisite standards. Well then, she would have a superstar in the family through marriage —daughter-in-law Liza whom, on the whole, Lucy averred, she liked a lot more than her son Desi. Lucy became very maternal with Liza.

'I felt like a mother to her before my children were

born, and I *know* her,' she told Charles Higham in the New York *Times*. 'Liza took on all the responsibility long before Judy died,' Lucy recalled. 'She helped Lorna Luft go out on her own. And now she has the responsibility of her half-brother, Joey Luft. I try to be a mother to her,' sighed mama Ball.

Liza had been mother to both Lorna and Joey. When Lorna was removed from the cast of *Lolita*, during its pre-Broadway shakedown, it was Liza who offered consolation and who helped her get readjusted. When Lorna then proved ready to enter the professional field of nightclub work, it was Liza who clucked proudly like a mother hen at the younger girl's club performances, attending whenever possible the opening nights until she discovered—or maybe, Lorna told her—she was stealing the spotlight from the star. Thereafter, Liza began adopting Mama's policy of attending second-night performances.

The half-sisters remain close and there seems to be no competitive spirit between them. Indeed, Lorna seems to be more Sid Luft's daughter than Judy Garland's and there is a quality of tough spunkiness about her that makes her seem more a threat for the audiences held by young Nancy Sinatra than for those that support Liza Minnelli.

Liza has kept Joey out of the limelight because he professes not to be seeking a show business career. She has financed his education in private schools and at college and has given him a home with her close friend and make-up artist Christina Smith and her husband.

Meanwhile, there was Liza's own career. She had another engagement at the Olympia Theatre in Paris, in a show that utilised for supporting acts Stephan Reggiani, The Edwardos, Trio Athenée, Italo, American Sunshine, and others. For the Parisians, Liza could do no wrong. *France-Soir* reported, 'Santa Claus, thank you, thank you for having already left this super present.' Another local journal wrote, 'A pontifical cascade of superlatives would not suffice to express the greatness of the talent and the personality of Liza Minnelli.'

After the Olympia evening, the Baron tossed an elite supper party for Liza, which he quaintly turned into a benefit for the United Jewish Appeal. Among the VIP guests at this resplendent event were Marie-Helene de Rothschild, Richard Burton and Elizabeth Taylor, Marisa Berenson, Yves St Laurent, Thierry van Zuylen, Countess Hubert d'Ornono, and selected other members of society's aristocrats. The celebration was held at the Baron's seventeenth-century Ile St Louis town house, a residence which could have been Liza's for the asking.

Then there was the world première of *Cabaret*. For the latter event, held at the new Zïegfeld Theatre in New York on February 13th, 1972, she was escorted by both Desi, Jnr, and Desi, Snr, but no Lucy.

The word was already out, however. There had been a mob scene at the first press preview at the Ziegfeld two nights before with two hundred guests, including the legendary 'man from the *New York Times*', left unseated. People were sitting on the steps in the loge and standing in the aisles but no amount of discomfort could dim their enthusiasm. The picture was good beyond expectation, and Liza was a smash, a sure-fire Academy Award nominee.

The critics were generally in accord that Liza was a sensation. There were a few dissenters, such as Andrew Sarris of *The Village Voice* who proclaimed, 'I have now endured Miss Minnelli in all of her previous filmic incarnations as the vulnerably ugly duckling, and I discover to my shame and sorrow that she has become entirely too conspicuous for my taste.' He went on to add that in *Cabaret* she comes '. . . crashing through with all the finesse of a water buffalo in heat. It is enough to make even such macho types as John Wayne and Clint Eastwood fall into each other's arms for comfort.'

But far more typical of the evaluations of Liza's on-camera musical debut was Roger Ebert's judgments for the *Chicago Sun-Times*. 'Sally is brought magnificently to the screen by Liza Minnelli, who plays her as a girl who's bought what the cabaret is selling. To her, the point is to laugh and sing and live forever in the moment. To refuse to take things seriously—even Naziism—and to relate with people only up to a certain point. She is capable of warmth and emotion, but a lot of it is theatrical, and when the chips are down she's as decadent as the "daringly decadent" dark fingernail polish she flaunts. Liza Minnelli plays Sally Bowles so well and fully that it doesn't matter how well she sings and dances, if you see what I mean.'

Yet Liza did sing and dance very well in *Cabaret*. Although the film cut ten songs from the Broadway version (some to be heard as only background music), composers Ebb and Kander outfitted three tunes especially for Liza: the already known *Maybe This Time* and two zippy numbers, *Mein Herr*, and *Money*,

Money, Money (sung in duet with devilish master of ceremonies Grey). Quite naturally, every moviegoer eagerly anticipated how Liza would handle the rendition of the climactic title tune. It emerged, as it rightly should, as a desperate plea, rather than a song of defiant happiness.

The enormous energies Liza demonstrated in her musical moments in *Cabaret* did lead a few critical voices, such as *Time* magazine's Jay Cocks, to air the feeling that the musical numbers failed because 'It is impossible to believe, once Liza starts singing, that this is a girl doomed to spend her career belting out tunes in third-rate clubs; her talents as a performer are simply too great for the part—and for the movie.'

Joseph Gelmis of *Newsday* seemed to have the final word on the subject, 'If you, like me, have been a Minnelli fan since her desperate gaiety of *The Sterile Cuckoo*, you will not have to make any allowances for her overpowering ways. She is what she is, and you either like her or you don't.'

Obviously the North American moviegoers adored Liza and *Cabaret*, for the film, which cost 4·25 million dollars to make, grossed over 18·175 million dollars on that continent alone while its wider success carried the name of Liza Minnelli round the globe and brought enormous financial rewards to Allied Artists Pictures.

With the smash opening of *Cabaret*, Liza found herself the next week adorning the covers of both *Time* and *Newsweek* magazines and the hastily contrived but lengthy stories inside would be virtual duplications, feeding the public what they wanted to read of this *wunderkind*.

Liza had been paid two hundred and fifty thousand

dollars for *Cabaret*. Now her price was climbing higher, much higher. Some offers exceeded one million dollars, the price which had seemed so outrageous when Elizabeth Taylor was claiming that fee at the peak of her box-office powers in the mid-1960s. But Liza rejected them all. She wanted to make a movie with her father, whose last film, *On a Clear Day You Can See Forever* (1970) with Barbra Streisand, had been such a let-down for all concerned.

Zelda, the story of Zelda Fitzgerald, from the book by Nancy Milford, seemed the ideal vehicle. However, it proved unavailable for Liza or for Jane Fonda, who also wanted to portray the outrageous prototype of the roaring twenties. Then Liza and Vincente decided on *The Last Flapper*, an F. Scott Fitzgerald story about a thinly disguised Zelda, but that, too, fell through, as well as the plan to team Liza with Robert Redford, who went on to appear with Liza's close friend Mia Farrow in another Fitzgerald work, *The Great Gatsby* (1974).

Minnelli and Liza finally settled on a bizarre Maurice Druon novel, *Film of Memory*, which they planned to call *Carmella* and which would have Katharine Hepburn as co-star. Terence Rattigan's script proved unacceptable and Frederic Raphael was assigned the task, everyone hoping he would turn out another *Darling* (1965) or *Two for the Road* (1967). By this time, Hepburn was out of the project and in early 1974 it was rumoured that silent screen star Pola Negri would make one of her periodic comebacks in the role originally intended for Hepburn. That, too, came to naught.

Liza, however, kept busy—publicly and privately.

On May 30th, Memorial Day, 1972, she attended a performance of *Jesus Christ, Superstar* at the Mark Hellinger Theatre in New York. She was particularly impressed by the dynamic young black performer who played Judas. His name: Ben Vereen. He also happened to be a protégé of Bob Fosse, as was Liza.

It was no time for socialising, however. The next evening she taped her television special, *Liza with a Z*, before an invited audience at the Lyceum Theatre. Not that it was needed, but an enthusiastic response from the assembled viewers was guaranteed—the audience having been plied with champagne in the theatre lobby before the performance. *Liza with a Z* was aired, to exceptional acclaim, by NBC on September 10th, 1972. *Variety* recorded, 'Miss Minnelli has shown in the past that she has great instincts for live performance and responds well to that form of entertainment. She has also too often shown a predilection for bringing to such performances a preoccupation with being her mother's daughter. Fosse and Ebb in *Liza* turned her more towards what seems to be her "own way" than has previously been shown on TV, and her response—especially her handling of the energetic dance requirements—was that of a great trouper on the brink of establishing her own distinctive mark in the show biz world.'

It seemed only the next day thereafter that Singer Sewing Machines, the sponsors of *Liza with a Z*, were selling the 'live' concert LP albums at special promotional prices in their national outlets.

In the summer of 1972, Liza followed Desi to Japan, where he was filming *Marco* at the Toho studios, and it was during production of this little-seen epic that the couple officially announced their engagement. Liza said, 'We won't get married for a while, but surely within the next few months.' But during the next few, presumably idyllic months, Liza began to feel that the romance was petering out.

The strain between the two became apparent to outsiders on January 19th, 1973, which was Desi's birthday. Liza threw a surprise party for Desi at Le Bistro, one of California's swingier joints. For a while the evening went smoothly. Then Liza wanted to dance. Desi refused to be her partner.

Afterwards, she explained her attitude to *Playgirl* magazine. 'Guys who won't let themselves go irk me,' Liza is quoted as saying. 'I'm an adventurer and I do things spontaneously. The night of Desi's birthday party I felt like doing some wild dancing, but Desi is more uptight than I and wouldn't dance, so he sat on the sidelines while I danced with another partner.'

A little more than a week later, on January 29th, Liza attended the Golden Globe Awards and received honours as 'Best Actress—Comedy or Musical' for her performance in *Cabaret*. Also present was twenty-year-old Edward Albert, son of Eddie Albert and Margo, accepting the award for 'Most Promising Male Newcomer' as a result of his performance on screen in *Butterflies Are Free*.

Liza found him more than promising. A new romance was born.

By now, Liza was gathering a sizeable number of show business awards. She had been named, along with Sammy Davis, Jnr, Entertainer of the Year, at the Second Annual Award dinner at the Las Vegas Hilton. (This prompted club owners in Las Vegas to bestow on Liza their heaviest tribute, putting her first name alone on the marquee when she played the gambling capital's nightclubs. It proved, by Vegas standards, that she was indeed a superstar.) In November of 1972, Liza went to Bal Harbour, Florida, to attend the National Association of Theatre Owners' convention and to accept their Star of the Year trophy.

By early 1973, Liza and Diana Ross (*Lady Sings the Blues*) were odds-on favourites to win the Best Actress Award at the Academy Awards. (Maggie Smith of *Travels with My Aunt*, Cicely Tyson of *Sounder*, and Liv Ullman of *The Emigrants* were the other nominees for the category that year.) The presentation of the Best Actress Award that evening, March 27th, at the Dorothy Chandler Pavilion, was preceded by the embarrassment of the Best Actor Award when Marlon Brando sent the former winner of MGMs *House of Dark Shadows* 'Miss Vampire' Contest, Sacheen Little-feather, on stage to reject his Oscar for *The Godfather* because of Hollywood's mistreatment of the American Indian.

This was followed by the indiscreet comments of presenter Clint Eastwood, suggesting that somebody should offer an award for all the cowboys killed by the Indians in John Ford movies, and then the strange and embarrassing spectacle of Raquel Welch, with Gene Hackman, presenting the Best Actress Award. As Hackman opened the envelope, Raquel tittered on about how dearly she liked all the ladies nominated, but how she hoped whoever won 'didn't have a cause'.

It was a tough act for Liza Minnelli, winner of the

year's award, to follow, especially after Hackman had commented on her breeding and blood lines, likening her to a thoroughbred race horse. Liza, in what may have been the evening's only display of good taste and intelligence, came demurely but radiantly to the podium, clutched the Oscar and said, 'Thank you very much for this award. You have made *me* very happy.'

Now having won a Tony and an Oscar, Liza would soon be a three medium winner, for she would be voted a television Emmy for her sparkling *Liza with a Z.*

If Mama could see her now!

CHAPTER SEVENTEEN

On May 11th, 1973, Liza opened at the Palladium in London. And at this point Peter Sellers entered her life.

The forty-seven-year-old comedian was in constant attendance during Liza's three Palladium shows and he literally swept her off her feet, as he had many women of varying ages and looks both before and after his marriage to actress Britt Eckland, the second of Sellers' three wives. 'He must have used one of his disguises on her,' quipped Britt.

A few days later, a glossy-eyed Liza was jubilantly announcing to a dutiful press, 'I fell in love with this man, and I am pleased to say that he fell in love with me.' Sellers said, 'We both believe in humour and in having good times. We haven't found anything that we disagree on.'

Sellers began talking about marriage once they were clear of their respective spouses. Back in California, Desi Jnr was fuming—publicly. 'Something has gone wrong, that's for sure. It all turned sour since

Liza went to England.' Mama Lucy would defensively add that Desi had at last discovered that you just cannot domesticate Liza.

Within five weeks, however, the Minnelli–Sellers romance was off. Sellers was left with nothing but memories of Liza and supposedly some photos for which he claims she had willingly posed.

Liza had a rather *laissez faire* attitude to romantic relationships, or so she persistently claimed in public. She told Rona Barrett in 1971, 'You sing another song and you find someone else. It's just like a marvellous circle. I think of people like—Oh, my God, there's so many people in the world to meet and to know and to ask.'

For Liza, in the coming months, love, with or without Desi, would be like a carousel.

When she left England, Liza informed the press about her time with funnyman Sellers: '. . . a lovely, lovely man . . . Yes, it's over . . . No, I have no regrets . . . How can you regret anything that was so happy?"

As the year progressed, the media seemed to turn to her for words of wisdom on a variety of subjects.

On stardom: 'I do have fears that being a star can get the best of you. But I have learned that you have to be careful. The more successful you get, the more you have to convince people around of your longevity. People tend to think this is it—what's happening now. But I didn't set out only to be a girl of the year. That's not what I want to do. It's terrific. But if you think of it only that way, there is a finality. There are 365 days to a year, and everything you do is different and what you build on the future is the answer.'

On fan magazines: 'If I'm standing with a doorman

157

waiting for a cab, and a photographer takes a picture, it winds up as a romance on the cover of a fan magazine. If I go to a movie with somebody, they say the romance I had with the doorman, or whoever I was standing with, is over when I never had one to start with. It's got to the point where I can't go to the movies anymore!'

By July of 1973, Liza was in Italy discussing with director Franco Zeffirelli the possibilities of her starring in a screen version of *Camille* to be set in the period of Toulouse-Lautrec. The film venture never came to fruition. In November, she was in Paris, participating in a fashion show for five American designers, a stellar event hostessed by Baroness Guy de Rothschild and lavishly arranged at the Palace of Versailles. Among those attending the gala were Princess Grace of Monaco, Rudolf Nureyev, Josephine Baker, Danielle Darrieux, and the usual array of continental blue bloods.

At this point in her career, Liza was considered very much a fashion plate. Even many people on the street knew that the usual Liza outfit included clothes from Halston, jewellery by Elsa Perette ('It's very striking to wear nothing but silver. So many people wear gold'), hair styles by Gus Lepre, make-up by Tina Fraker, and false eyelashes by Christina Smith. The oversized eyelashes have become Liza's trademark. 'They're kinda outrageous, but I can get away with it.'

Back in the United States, Liza resumed her concert tours and made plans for an engagement at the Winter Garden Theatre in New York.

The new man in her life was Broadway success and Tony winner Ben Vereen, the black star of *Pippin*. However, Liza maintained that they were merely good friends. They were still good friends in February, 1974, when Ben accompanied her to Rio and when a 'brotherhood' photograph showing Vereen clutching Liza's presumably bared breasts was printed in *Newsweek* magazine. Offstage they were 'on', frequently performing impromptu song-and-dance routines (just as she and Peter Allen once had) at some of the more permissive bars in the shadows of the Gay White Way.

For Liza, the upcoming Winter Garden engagement was especially important. Hitherto, one-woman shows on Broadway had been concert presentations or elongated vaudeville turns in the old 'Judy at the Palace' tradition.

That was not for Liza. At fifteen dollars per seat, the carelessly conceived Garland style of engagement would be a public rip-off, she believed. Liza wanted to present a full-scale, professionally choreographed and directed *tour de force* that would knock critics and audiences for a loop. *She*, Liza Minnelli, would give them their money's worth and *she* had proved she could do it with her one-woman show at the Palladium.

Typically, Liza set out to bring new life to Broadway by deliberately underselling herself. She did not want to appear at the Palace, she said, or at Carnegie Hall *until* she had a *whole* new act. This one was not new, for it was just her nightclub routine combined with some TV specialities. *The Best of Liza Minnelli* you might call it. Most of the critics took the hint and, on opening night, declared that it was not only the best of Liza Minnelli but the best of Broadway.

The 1,442-seat Winter Garden was the ideal theatre for Liza's assault on critics who usually concerned themselves with lavish Broadway musicals or the latest obscurities from Edward Albee, Tennessee Williams, and Tom Stoppard. Rich in show business tradition, it had housed some of Broadway's biggest musical hits, including *Funny Girl* and *Mame*. It was the literal home of the show business superstars. Al Jolson enjoyed his greatest triumphs at the Winter Garden . . . as had Fannie Brice, W. C. Fields and, more recently, in a record-breaking engagement that would be broken (of course) by Liza, that singing poet of the rock generation, Neil Diamond. The Winter Garden, somehow, was always associated with 'where it's at' in the entertainment scene. Also, Liza was quick to remind reporters, it had been the scene of her father's early theatrical triumphs.

The Palace, on the other hand, was not the home of the reigning superstars. It had legendarily been the refuge of the faded vaudevillians and the home of the comeback artists. Some, like Garland and Danny Kaye, made it. Others, like Betty Hutton, did not.

The Palace, once the house of royalty for vaudeville, had long ago (as early as the advent of talking pictures in the late 1920s) fallen on the same hard times that distinguished many of its artists. Through everchanging managements, it had been a vaudeville stand, movie and stage show 'double feature' house (eclipsed, inevitably, by the bigger names playing at the Roxy, Paramount, and Strand), road show movie theatre (*Goodbye, Mr Chips*), second run movie house, legitimate Broadway theatre (*Sweet Charity, Applause*), and perennial showplace for the down-and-out, up-and-coming, or overnight sensation. No, the Palace was definitely not for Liza.

Then she learned that the one current entertainment

phenomenon who was even more the rage, more contemporary and, at the time, even hotter a name with New York audiences than Liza Minnelli, had signed for an engagement at, of all places, the Palace. It was Bette Midler, the new *super* superstar.

Liza Minnelli, herself a Divine Miss M., was at a distinct disadvantage. The added super in Bette's superstardom was due to best-selling recordings like *Boogie Woogie Bugle Boy* whereas Liza had *never* had a really solid-selling single platter.

Liza could have competed against Streisand. Barbra had not had a big hit record in a long time, though ironically by the time Liza concluded her engagement at the Winter Garden, Streisand, too, would be back on the pop charts with *The Way We Were*, the 'sleeper' song written by Liza's close friend Marvin Hamlisch for the movie which had been on release some months before the song caught on.

Bette Midler, the newest queen of the camp crowd, sold out her two-week engagement at the Palace within a week of the first announcement. 'Record-breaking,' said the keepers of such trivia.

When, a few weeks later, Liza's three-week-long engagement at the Winter Garden was announced, every available seat was sold within thirty-six hours of the first ticket sale. 'Fraud,' cried a public too long bilked by publicists attempting to create a demand for tickets to shows that in reality had little advance sale. But, in Liza's case, they soon discovered that the claims were not false. Every performance *was* sold out. There simply were no more seats available and soon the everpresent scalpers were demanding up to fifty dollars for a single ticket to the Minnelli show.

It was perfect—except for the impending threat of Bette Midler who, still, could ruin all of Liza's Broadway plans. Midler opened to generally enthusiastic reviews. Her reputation had preceded her and if her free-form performance, backed up by a trio of off-beat gals called The Harlots, lacked the professionalism that main stream critics preferred, it offered in substitute the sort of energy and desire to please that had been too seldom seen on Broadway. If not the ultimate in show business artistry that theatre patrons had long been seeking, Midler and company at least offered an nfectious blend of *chutzpah*, verve, and a wild, wicked wit.

If Bette Midler achieved perhaps more than she legitimately deserved in her Palace debut, Liza Minnelli would achieve more. Liza attended Midler's closing performance, December 23rd, an Actors' Fund Benefit, accompanied by 'friend' Chris Wallace, whom the star's clique insisted was *not* a boyfriend. Liza must have realised then how little there was to fear from comparison with her red-headed rival who, incidentally, would reciprocate by purchasing tickets to Liza's closing performance at the Winter Garden, but Bette would never make it to the theatre.

Even the ticket stubs for the Minnelli–Winter Garden stand would become collectors' items. By accident or design and, despite the inevitable inclusion on the bill of the song *Liza with a Z*, the admission ducats declared the attraction to be 'Lisa Minnelli'. They spelled her name correctly, however, on the giant billboard above the theatre.

The pivotal backstage staff for Liza's New York engagement consisted of her closest pals. Deanna

Wenble added to her chores the task of stage managing the 117 light cues for the shows. When Christina Smith arrived from Los Angeles and said that she had to return to California almost immediately (she was opening her own make-up shop on the coast), Nancy Barr was recruited to help the superstar with her quick changes for the one-woman show. When Nancy was not grabbing Liza's discarded tambourine, shoving a black sweater (Halston, of course) in the direction of the frenetic performer, or setting out an aqua robe in the dressing room, she was lining up audiences for the devout members of the Limelight for Liza, some of whom had travelled great distances to bestow gifts on their loved one. The always 'on' Liza always managed to be 'real' when dealing with this special segment of her fans.

In fact, Liza would go to great lengths to display her compassion for the inner circle of Liza Minnelli devotees. For example, when she was told that a club member was suffering from brain cancer and had unfavourable odds against surviving, the celebrity placed a call to the ailing twenty-two-year-old girl. The two chatted, with the girl constantly apologising for having taken up Liza's time. The next day, after the member underwent surgery, Liza again telephoned the hospital. Finally Liza was informed the girl had survived surgery. 'She made it!' Liza screamed to friends. Later, the now-recovered fan visited her idol several times backstage at the Winter Garden.

Liza's show at the Winter Garden opened in the manner that climaxed most star acts of the past. No warm-up troupers of the sort that have long kept experienced theatregoers from attending such shows until *after* the interval. Bette Midler, too, had broken with this tradition at the *beginning* of the evening but in the first post-intermission segment she reverted to form by giving a solo slot to her pianist-conductor, Barry Manilow.

With Liza's show, though, it was Liza—or record facsimile—all the way. A twenty-eight-piece orchestra, situated on stage midst a deep blue background, presented the illusion of limitless space. Jack French, the 'Silver Fox', was on hand to conduct the musicians. Framing each end of the stage were monolith-like speakers, the type which have in recent years become *de rigeur* for the younger artists, who feel that hand microphones fail to offer sufficiently real fidelity. They, and most especially Liza, do continue to use these mikes for dramatic effects that range from whiplashing the cord to making phallic attempts at becoming one with the instrument like Judy Garland or Linda Lovelace. The hand mike may have lost its practical value for today's entertainer but it has not lost its theatrical purpose.

Liza opened her evening with a show-stopper, an energetic song called *Say Yes*, and then she moved into a rendition of Stevie Wonder's *You and I*, a number that proved she had not lost touch with contemporary musical trends. Six more numbers followed, the actual selections varying during the show's final week in order to supply fresh material, not previously recorded, for the *Liza at the Winter Garden* LP album/cassette/tape. Next, four dancers—each surprisingly nimble—joined her on stage for a quartet of frantic dance numbers in which it became apparent that the star was lip-synching her vocals to a recorded track. It was a Broadway first

—and some traditionalist observers hoped it also would be a Broadway last.

During the course of the evening, with its single interval, Liza seemingly never stopped, pummelling the patrons with song after song and dance after dance. Occasionally she would sit on a stool to recapture her breath, but never lost the frantic pacing which is so much a part of her 'on' personality. She utilised clever patter to bridge the song numbers and to assure the audience that, though she may perspire a lot onstage, she is really having a good time and that she is happiest when she is pleasing the audience. As always, her salesladyship worked. There were few in the audience who were not fully enthralled with the ingratiating, effervescent Liza.

Most of the professional critics found Liza's show fresh, original, and vibrant, and labelled her the most exciting performer to hit the Big Apple in many years. Robert J. Landry declared in *Variety*, 'Not just a song and dance girl but also an actress, getting a lot of her effects facially and through body English, she has a piquant mixture of confidence and diffidence, of wham and subtlety. . . . Everything hung together. The faithful were not disappointed. The squares gave in The engineered hot rod pace never slackened. It was show business at its professional best.'

A little less impressed was Douglas Watt (*New York Daily News*) who took occasion to review her costumes, although he failed to mention her scene-stealing pink chiffon flowing scarf. 'Miss Minnelli comes to us in black and white. Besides the extremely attractive velvet little boy suit, she wears a grayish metallic gown, cut above the knees in front and sweeping the floor in back, and a shiny black mini-skirted dress for some of her nimble dancing.' As for her allure, Watt concluded, 'Winning though she is, Miss Minnelli's turn palls long before it is over as the carefully manufactured aura of triumph becomes cloying. She is brimming with health, energy and enthusiasm, and she is undeniably talented. Now all she needs is a little fresh air.'

Interestingly, little direct comment was made on two intriguing elements of Liza's show-stopping performance. One is that, contrary to public assumption, nothing of the Minnelli ambience, not one gesture, laugh, or bit of vocal phrasing, is left to chance. Like Marlene Dietrich, Liza pre-programmes every element of her performance, and if one should see her go through her paces on different nights, each song and every ounce of chatter is duplicated. The second fascinating aspect of Liza's footlight persona is that, unlike her late Mama, Liza seemingly cannot and will not cope with tactile audience response. When at the end of Liza's evening, loyal fans trooped down front, Liza onstage literally shrank back with unmasked fear, shying away from the mass of hands that reached up to touch, pat, or acknowledge adulation. This apprehension of fan crowds usually leads Liza to pull any sort of stunt to avoid the after-the-show lingerers who wish autographs, want to chat, or just to see their idol 'in real life'.

Throughout her Winter Garden engagement, Liza remained the talk of the town. After all, her Broadway presentation grossed 413,815 dollars, which was something of a record, as was her special midnight performance on Friday, January 25th, a benefit for the Actors' Fund. This event brought in an enormous sum for the charity: 21,040 dollars. If audience members that evening wondered what a special crew in the rear of the orchestra were about, it was simply to video tape Liza's 'historical' appearance at the Winter Garden. The film would be housed at the archives of the Lincoln Centre Library for the Performing Arts, with half the costs for this lensing absorbed by Liza. (She had got the brain storm for this project the week before when she, Ebb and Kander did a video tape interview at the Library for the Performing Arts.)

After the thunderous finale applause about 2 a.m. the Benefit audience was treated to a scene of dubious pleasure. Rotund Clive Barnes of the *New York Times* pivoted on stage and presented Liza with a special citation from the Actors' Fund. (Bette Midler had received one too.) Barnes became so enthralled in reciting his verbal tribute to the performer, that his five-minute speech snowballed into a miniature filibuster. A far less conspicuous attender that memorable evening was Ben Vereen, who slipped into his orchestra aisle seat after the lights had dimmed. During intermission he rushed backstage.

Four days after the Winter Garden closing, on January 30th, Liza was appearing at the Riviera Hotel in Las Vegas, and from there it was to Rio de Janeiro, where she played a week-long engagement and fell under the spell of handsome young Brazilian playboy Pedrinho Aquinaga. In next to no time, Liza was announcing her engagement and intention to give up her career to become a housewife. Not just any housewife. She would be the bride of the dashing swain who recently had been chosen as 'the most beautiful man in Brazil'.

But Liza returned to the United States alone and made plans to record a new album, a collection of original songs which she hoped would help her break into the 'singles' market and which would give her the same kind of teeny-bopper adulation enjoyed by Mick Jagger, Carly Simon, James Taylor, and Alice Cooper —most especially, Alice Cooper.

It meant another change of image for Liza, but it was a gradual change, one she had been planning for some time. An impromptu performance before a group of college students at the Hasty Pudding Club at Harvard where she accepted a 'Woman of the Year' award, had turned her on to the youth market.

Alice Cooper, the politically and—some say— morally conservative young man who sought and achieved notoriety and fame with a bizarre 'glitter' rock act he claimed had been inspired by the decadent musical numbers performed by Joel Grey in the screen version of *Cabaret*, was the star best suited to help Liza reach her new audience. Only it had to be done slowly, so that she did not lose the fans she had already gained.

But the relationship would be strictly friendship and business, no romance—so Liza and Alice maintained. Suddenly, Liza's concert appearances were being promoted on 'top 40' radio stations by Alice, who promised to appear on the bill with her in New Haven. It brought in crowds where none had been anticipated, the kind of crowds that usually turn out for The Rolling Stones, James Brown, Taylor and Simon. Liza, tentatively, was on her way towards establishing a new image. She even appeared as back-up singer on Alice's record album, *Muscle of Love*, for Warner Bros records.

Typically, the new image that Liza would pick for

herself would be different from anything one might expect from someone determined to crack the youth barriers. She would become Liza Minnelli—madcap Lucky Lady, last of the flappers and free spirits, a gal of the roaring twenties transferred to today. The world wanted fun and Liza would be a 'fun' person.

It was probably a smart move. Nostalgia was 'in'— *The Sting*, the Gatsby Look, rinky-tink tunes by Paul McCartney—and now, Liza to be the living embodiment of it all. As Sally Bowles would have said, 'It is all too, too divine.'

That week in Rio with 'the most beautiful man in Brazil' had got her new image off to a rousing start. Meanwhile the 'old' Liza was fading unobtrusively into the background even as she appeared in public. There was an awkward and forgettable performance on the Oscar show, in April, singing an original song devoted to the Academy Awards, and, on April 30th, a long-postponed and horrendous television special with Charles Aznavour that received little promotion and very low ratings.

The public saw the 'new' Liza 'live' on the Tony Awards show, telecast on April 21st, when she accepted a plaque for her Winter Garden performance in ebullient, gushy, infectious style that was meant to exhibit her carefree razzamatazz—'razzamatazz' and 'pzzazz' were now among Liza's favourite words. Then, in mid-May, she joined with others on the stage of the Palace Theatre (she finally 'played' there) in a tribute to Jule Styne. She sang *I Guess I'll Have to Hang My Tears out to Dry* from *Glad to See You*, and *Some People* from *Gypsy*. This evening proved, as had the earlier Jim Stacy Benefit in March in Hollywood, that these days no show business charity show is complete without Liza's participation. She not only is in the main stream of the profession's 'in' crowd, she seems to be its very centre.

And, of course, there was another new man in her life, Jack Haley, Jnr, ageing (forty-one) Hollywood Lothario and producer of *That's Entertainment* (1974), the movie musical compendium in which Liza appeared as a guest star and narrator. He had swept Liza off her feet. They quickly became 'engaged'.

'I believe every girl should be engaged to marry Jack Haley, Jnr, at least once in her lifetime,' quipped *The Hollywood Reporter* columnist Hank Grant, who had previously chronicled the seemingly publicity-hungry Haley's affairs with Carol Lynley and Nancy Sinatra, Jnr.

Yes, Liza said, she was marrying Haley.

No, Liza said, she was not marrying Haley.

Well, maybe.

Maybe, she might even get that long-planned divorce from Peter Allen.

Then again, maybe not. After all, claimed Liza, 'I'm married to my career.'

She would make up her mind after vacationing on the Riviera with Haley. And Liza needed a vacations Earlier that spring, the girl who seemingly existed on Zagnut candy bars and chocolate milk drinks, had contracted 'flu during her engagement at Harrah's Club in Lake Tahoe, Nevada. (Contrary to the rumour that she had collapsed on stage or in the wings at the casino, her local physician had ordered the star to recuperate in bed for a day, and she had taken the evening of April 15th off.)

Coincidentally, Liza was one of the many show business celebrities defrauded by the bankrupt Home-Stake Productions Company of Tulsa, Oklahoma. Her pal Candice Bergen had been a victim, as had Martin Bregman, her financial adviser. Liza's investment was reported at 231,000 dollars.

Fiddle-de-dee. It's only money. It's carnival time in Europe . . . and awaa-ay we go. There were stopovers in Nice at the Leslie Bricusses' home, plus a special invitation from Prince Rainier and Princess Grace to attend the June 22nd Monaco gala charity affair headlining Sammy Davis, Jnr. Liza and Jack Haley would make an appearance at the splashy evening festivities, but Sammy Davis, Jnr, would not. (He insisted that his non-show was in retaliation for the alleged slights to his wife Altovise by the royal couple.)

Meanwhile, back in New York, the almost-ignored Peter Allen filed for divorce from Liza. Insiders insisted that the delicate question of a satisfactory property settlement had long delayed this step on Allen's part. Now Liza and Haley, Jnr, began to be more specific about their wedding plans. It would occur, it all went well, in the fall.

Refreshed by her European holiday, Liza returned to her taxing schedule of live performances. On Wednesday, July 10th, she opened at the Riviera in Las Vegas. The marquee in front of the oversized casino-hotel simply stated 'LIZA'. It was sufficient to ensure a sold-out two-week engagement. Her act was still much the same as when she had performed at the Winter Garden Theatre. While some reviewers complained that it was time for Liza to freshen up her material and expand her horizons, the crowds were pleased by her show routine. As the *Daily Variety* stringer would report of the occasion, 'She has become the total mesmerizer, her performances moving to near-perfection.'

While ringsiders were being enraptured by Liza on-stage, a more intriguing, bubbly show was occurring in the club's wings. Before this latest Riviera opening, Liza had called Papa in California and insisted that he must attend on the 10th. She instructed him that he was not to come to the first show, but to the midnight edition. She further explained to Papa that he was to dine first with his fiancée, Lee Anderson, and the Jack Haleys (senior and wife and junior). Then they were all to come backstage *after* the show.

The ever-obliging Vincente did just as he was instructed. Once backstage, Jack, Jnr, formally asked Minnelli for permission to wed Liza.

In his soft yet dramatic voice Vincente responded, 'No!'

The exuberant look of expectation on Liza's face suddenly changed to one of disappointment. 'Oh, Daddy, how can you say that?'

'Oh, baby, I was only kidding, you know.'

Joy reigned again for Miss Superstar.

The day after Liza completed her engagement at the Riviera, Peter Allen, on Tuesday, July 24th, appeared in Manhattan Supreme Court to obtain the divorce. Liza was not present at the brief proceedings. Later that evening, Peter popped up at the Grand Finale Club on West 70th Street to see Daphne Davis impersonate Liza in a 'drag' act. He was reported ecstatic, which is more than his pals said he was about the termination of his domestic relationship with Liza.

When asked about Liza's proposed marriage to Jack Haley, Jnr, a benign Peter commented, 'I only know what I read in the papers.' When queried why he was finally getting a divorce after all this time, he merely shrugged and said, 'When you've been separated longer than you were married, it's time to get a divorce.' Did he feel that being wed to a superstar had eclipsed his own career? He said no. 'I found out I was a writer rather than a performer.' He did throw in a plug for a new album of his own songs which he was then preparing. 'I wanted to call it *Overnight Success*, but I've settled on *Just Ask Me, I've Been There*.'

That Liza was somewhat overwhelmed by the notion of wedding for a second time was revealed by the quality of her serious responses to the press while fielding questions on the subject of matrimony. 'I want a man who is gentle and kind and has a good sense of humour, is intelligent, fun to be with—somebody you'd like to spend your time with,' she admitted to reporters, while glancing over at Haley, who was in attendance at this particular press conference.

Compatibility with a man was now not the only requisite for Liza, particularly if they were contemplating having children. 'If somebody loves you, they give you their name. It's about all they've got in the long run. I believe in tradition. I was born in tradition. My parents were very romantic.' As if to emphasise the fact that the 'new' Liza was going to be very respectable indeed, she added, 'Marriage is important for people who want children.'

Evidently, becoming a mother was very much on Liza's mind. On another occasion when she chatted with the press, the once free-wheeling young lady ruminated, 'I got married as a girl and I never really understood the consequences of my actions. We [she and Peter Allen] were like two kids, playing at life. I never once thought about children, because I was one myself. . . . Around the time I began to feel I was ready it was too late.'

Despite her reflective mood, Liza had several professional engagements to honour. After performing in Allentown, Pennsylvania in early August, she and Jack Haley, Jnr, went to Marbella, Spain, where she appeared at the August-Beach Club for three days. Then it was back to North America and a show at the Canadian National Exposition in Toronto. Then Liza had a day off. It was only a breather for she thereafter embarked on rapid-fire succeeding performances at the Minnesota, Iowa, Indiana, and Ohio State Fairs from August 23rd to the 28th.

After a guest spot on Johnny Carson's *Tonight Show* on August 30th to help Papa promote his autobiography and Jack, Jnr, to plug *That's Entertainment*, Liza actually devoted two full weeks to preparing for that wedding-in-the-future, which she and Haley had now actually scheduled for September 15th.

Cynics doubted the 'blessed' event would ever come to pass. Even on that special Sunday, scoffers were sure that Liza would find some reason for backing out of the personal commitment. When the bride-to-be failed to appear at the El Monecito Presbyterian Church at the appointed hour, pessimists began mouthing 'I told you so.' But, although nearly sixty minutes late, Liza eventually did make her appearance at the Spanish-style church located in the coastal village of Monecito, some ninety miles from Hollywood. Breathlessly, she rushed into the chapel, dressed in a bright yellow silk Halston pantsuit, with a triple-layered yellow chiffon blouse, decorated with a garland necklace of gold and diamonds. She carried a bouquet of yellow daisies. Before the actual ceremony took place, Liza showed guests the gold bracelet set with diamonds that Jack had given her. Inscribed on it were the words, 'I offer you all my worldly goods, my name and my heart.'

There was only a small, select group of friends and relatives present at the nuptials. Sammy Davis, Jnr and his wife Altovise served as best man and matron of honour. Although the ceremony was conducted by Judge John Griffin of Beverly Hills, it was Liza who composed her own special vows *à la* Ali McGraw of *Love Story*. As she nervously knelt before the altar, she spoke forth, 'You multiply my joy, you divide my grief, you are my love, my companion and my dearest friend.' Then after a brief benediction, Judge Griffin pronounced the couple man and wife.

The service itself only required twelve minutes, but it was the climax to long months of expectation. As Sammy Davis, Jnr, jokingly, but yet seriously remarked as the newlyweds left the chapel, 'Man, are we happy we got this done!'

Later that day, the couple entertained a less intimate gathering of guests at their Beverly Hills abode. Among those present were Gene Kelly, Yul Brynner, Ricardo Montalban, and Tony Franciosa. The bridal couple disappeared early from the festivities, visiting the home of Haley's parents close by.

The next evening, the couple were the subject of an old-fashioned Hollywood bash held at the former

Ciro's nightclub on Sunset Boulevard. The entertainment spot, now called Art Loboe's, was the stopping-off place for six hundred 'pals' of Liza and Jack, Jnr. The guest list read like a Who's Who of the show business colony, ranging from Johnny Carson to Elizabeth Taylor to Alice Cooper and on to Fred Astaire and Shirley MacLaine, Zsa Zsa Gabor, Fran and Edgar Bergen, Roger Smith and Ann-Margret, Alana and George Hamilton, Jack Benny, Milton Berle, Peter Lawford, Rita Hayworth, David Bowie, and of course, the two reigning queens of the gossip columns, Rona Barrett and Joyce Haber. The Jack Haley, Snrs, Vincente Minnelli, and the Sammy Davis, Jnrs, were the hosts for this extravagant fiesta that some ranked only second to the Annual Ball following the Oscar telecast. The sole catastrophe of the evening occurred when Liza cut the wedding cake and got icing dabbled all over her elbow-length white leather gloves. The misadventure was enough to launch Liza on to a crying ag and she ran into the ladies' room, where she remained until persuaded to re-emerge to mingle with the assemblage. 'Oh, it's just because I'm so happy onight,' she explained to overly concerned friends, and soon the episode was all but forgotten.

For their honeymoon, the couple combined business with pleasure. They vacationed in London where *That's Entertainment* just happened to be making its bow.

It would be nice to assume that having found connubial bliss, Liza could taper off her professional career and concentrate on being a wife first and foremost. But she is too much of a trouper to drop out of the race. She—not to mention those around her—has invested too much time and energy building her name into a marquee value to let it all go to waste now.

As she indicated in her on-camera spot in *That's Entertainment*, she is tremendously aware of the impermanence of fame and wants to preserve her peak years on film. She negotiated a two-picture pact with United Artists and also agreed to make *Lucky Lady* with, possibly, Burt Reynolds at Twentieth Century-Fox. (A short time later it was announced that Jack Haley, Jnr, had been selected as the new chief of TV at Twentieth Century-Fox Television.) Evidently, Fox expects big returns on Liza's new film, for the husband-and-wife team of Willard Huyck and Gloria Katz who created *American Graffiti* were paid four hundred thousand dollars for their scenario of rum-running in the 1920s which will be filmed largely in South America. Hollywood's master of madcap sophistication, Stanley Donen, is to direct the film.

So say goodbye to Sally Bowles and say hello to carefree Lucky Lady Liza. The girl once known as the 'determined hoyden' has a new role to play in life, a new fantasy to fulfil so that the real Liza can remain forever hidden from herself.

Lucky lady?

FILMOGRAPHY

IN THE GOOD OLD SUMMERTIME (*Metro-Goldwyn-Mayer, 1949*)
   Colour—102 minutes
   Producer, Joe Pasternak; director, Robert Z. Leonard; based on the play *Parfumerie* by Miklos Laszlo; original screenplay, Samsom Raphaelson; new screenplay, Albert Hackett, Frances Goodrich, Ivan Tors; art directors, Cedric Gibbons, Randall Duell; songs: *Merry Christmas* by Janice Torre and Fred Spielman; *Meet Me Tonight in Dreamland* by Beth Slater Whitson and Lee Friedman; *Put Your Arms Around Me Honey* by Junie McCree and Harry Von Tilzer; *Play that Barber Shop Chord* by Ballard MacDonald, William Tracey, and Lewis Muir; *I Don't Care* by Jean Lenox and Harry Sutton; music director, George Stoll; camera, Harry Stradling; editor, Adrienne Fazan.
   Judy Garland (Veronica Fisher); Van Johnson (Andrew Larkin); S. Z. Sakall (Otto Oberkugen); Spring Byington (Nellie Burke); Clinton Sundberg (Rudy Hansen); Buster Keaton (Hickey); Marcia Van Dyke (Louise Parkson); Lillian Bronson (Aunt Addie); Liza Minnelli (Veronica and Andrew's daughter); Joy Lansing, Bette Arlen (Pretty Girls); Howard Mitchell (Cop); Constance Purdy (Gushing Woman); Antonio Filauri (Italian Proprietor); Anna Q. Nilsson (Woman with Harp); Chester Clute (Man with Sheet Music); Eula Guy (Bird-Like Woman); Albert Moran (Waiter); Joan Welles (Susie); Jack Roth (Orchestra Leader); Peggy Leon, Frank Mayo (Guests).

JOURNEY BACK TO OZ (a.k.a. RETURN TO OZ) (*Filmation, 1962*)
   Colour—88 minutes
   Producers, Norman Prescott, Lou Scheimer; associate producers, Fred Ladd, Preston Blair; director, Hal Sutherland; based on characters created by L. Frank Baum; screenplay, Ladd, Prescott; additional dialogue, Bernard Evslin; sequence directors, Rudy Larriva, D. Towsley; songs, Sammy Cahn and Jimmy Van Heusen; music

director, Walter Scharf; animator, Amby Paliwoda; art director, Christensen; sound effects, Horta-Mahana Corp.; camera, Sergio Antonio Akcazar; supervising editor, Joseph Simon.

Voices of: Milton Berle (The Cowardly Lion); Herschel Bernardi (Woodenhead/The Horse); Paul Ford (Uncle Henry); Margaret Hamilton (Aunt Em); Jack E. Leonard (The Signpost); Paul Lynde (Pumpkinhead); Ethel Merman (Mombi, the Bad Witch); Liza Minnelli (Dorothy); Mickey Rooney (The Scarecrow); Rise Stevens (Glinda, the Good Fairy); Danny Thomas (The Tinman); Mel Blanc (The Crow).

CHARLIE BUBBLES (*Regional, 1968*) Colour—89 minutes

Producer, Michael Medwin; associate producer, George Pitcher; director, Albert Finney; screenplay, Shelagh Delaney; art director, Ted Marshall; set decorator, Jose Macavin; music director, Misha Donat; assistant director, Terence Clegg; sound, Peter Handford; camera, Peter Suschitsky; editor, Fergus McDonnell.

Albert Finney (Charlie Bubbles); Billie Whitelaw (Lottie); Colin Blakely (Smokey Pickles); Liza Minnelli (Eliza); Timothy Garland (Jack); Richard Pearson (The Accountant); John Ronane (Gerry); Nicholas Phipps (Agent); Peter Sallis (Lawyer); Charles Lamb (Mr Noseworthy); Margery Mason (Mrs Noseworthy); Diana Coupland (Maud); Alan Lake (Airman); Yootha Joyce, Peter Carlisle, Wendy Padbury (People in Motorway Café); Susan Engle (The Nanny); Joe Gladwin (Waiter in Hotel); Charles Hill (Headwaiter); Albert Shepherd (Policeman); Ted Morris (Bill); Bryan Moseley (Herbert); Rex Boyd (Receptionist).

THE STERILE CUCKOO (*Paramount, 1969*) Colour—107 minutes

Executive producer, David Lange; producer-director, Alan J. Pakula; based on the novel by John Nichols; screenplay, Alvin Sargent; music, Fred Karlin; song, *Come Saturday Morning* by Karlin and Dory Previn; art director, Roland Anderson; set decorator, Charles Pierce; costumes, Jennifer

Parsons (ladies), John Anderson (men); make-up, Mike Moschella; assistant director, Don Kranze; sound, Benjamin Winkler, John Muchmore, John Wilkinson; special effects, Charles Spurgeon; camera, Milton R. Krasner; editors, Sam O'Steen, John W. Wheeler.

Liza Minnelli (Mary Anne 'Pookie' Adams); Wendell Burton (Jerry Payne); Tim McIntire (Charlie Schumaker); Elizabeth Harrower (Landlady); Austin Green (Pookie's Father); Sandra Faison (Nancy Putnam); Chris Bugbee (Roe); Jawn McKinley (Helen Upshaw); and: Fred M. Lerner, A. Frederick Gooseen, Mark P. Fish, Philip S. Derfler, John A. Hussey, Toni Shorrock, Eric Best, Becky Davis, Towyna Thomas, Frances Tobin, Tim Laurie, Margaret Markov, Anita Alberts, Warren Peterson, Paul McConnell, Adele Wynn, Cynthia Hull.

TELL ME THAT YOU LOVE ME, JUNIE MOON (*Paramount, 1970*)
    Colour—112 minutes
    Producer, Otto Preminger; associate producer, Nat Rudich; director, Preminger; based on the novel by Marjorie Kellogg; screenplay, Kellogg; assistant director, Norman Cook; music, Philip Springer; songs: *Old Devil Time* by Pete Seeger; *Elvira* by Pacific Gas and Electric; *The Rake* and *Work Your Show* by Springer and Estelle Levitt; wardrobe designers, Ron Talsky, Phyllis Gart; make-up, Charles Schram; set director, Morris Hoffman; sound, Ben Winkler, Franklin Milton; camera, Boris Kaufman; editors, Henry Berman, Dean O. Ball.

Liza Minnelli (Junie Moon); Ken Howard (Arthur); Robert Moore (Warren); James Coco (Mario); Kay Thompson (Gregory); Fred Williamson (Beach Boy); Ben Piazza (Jesse); Emily Yancy (Solans); Leonard Frey (Guiles); Clarice Taylor (Minnie); James Beard (Sidney Wyner); Julie Bovasso (Ramona); Gina Collins (Lila); Barbara Logan (Mother Moon); Nancy Marchand (Nurse Oxford); Lynn Milgrim (Nurse Holt); Ric O. Feldman (Joebee); James D. Pasternak (Artist); Angelique Pettyjohn (Melissa); Anne Revere (Miss Farber); Elaine Shore (Mrs

Wyner); Guy Sorel (Dr Gaines); Wayne Tippett (Dr Miller); Pacific Gas and Electric (Themselves).

CABARET (*ABC Pictures—Allied Artists, 1972*) Colour—118 minutes
Producer, Cy Feuer; associate producer, Harold Nebenzal; director-choreography, Bob Fosse; based on the musical play by Joe Masteroff, the play *I Am a Camera* by John Van Druten and the book *Goodbye to Berlin* by Christopher Isherwood; screenplay, Jay Presson Allen; production designer, Rolf Zehetbauer; art director, Jurgen Kiebach; set decorator, Herbert Strabl; assistant directors, Douglas Green, Wolfgang Glattes; music, John Kander, lyrics, Fred Ebb; songs: *Willkommen, Mein Herr, Two Ladies, Maybe This Time I'll Be Lucky, Money, Money, Money, If You Could See Her Through My Eyes, Tomorrow Belongs to Me, Cabaret, Finale,* and: *Heiraten* (recorded by Greta Keller) and *Tiller Girls* (instrumental); musical director-orchestrator, Ralph Burns; music co-ordinator, Raoul Kraushaar; choreography assistant, John Sharpe; costumes, Charlotte Flemming; make-up and hairstyles, Raimund Stangl, Susi Krause; Liza Minnelli's hairstyles, Gus Le Pre; sound, David Hildyard, Robert Knudson, Arthur Piantadosi; camera, Geoffrey Unsworth; editor, David Bretherton.
Liza Minnelli (Sally Bowles); Michael York (Brian Roberts); Helmut Griem (Maximilian von Heune); Joel Grey (Master of Ceremonies); Fritz Wepper (Fritz Wendel); Marisa Berenson (Natalie Landauer); Elisabeth Neumann-Viertel (Fraulein Schneider); Sigrid Von Richthofen (Fraulein Mayr); Helen Vita (Fraulein Kost); Gerd Vespermann (Bobby); Ralf Wolter (Herr Ludwig); Georg Hartmann (Willi); Ricky Renee (Elkee); Estrongo Nachama (Cantor); Louise Quick (Gorilla); Kathryn Doby, Inge Jaeger, Angelika Koch, Helen Velkovorska, Gitta Schmidt, Louise Quick (Kit-Kat Dancers).

181

THAT'S ENTERTAINMENT (*United Artists, 1974*) Colour—132
  minutes

Executive producer, Daniel Melnick; producer-director-
scripter, Jack Haley, Jnr; additional music adaptor, Henry
Mancini; music supervisor, Jesse Kaye; assistant directors,
Richard Bremerkamp, David Silver, Claude Binyon, Jnr;
film librarian, Mort Feinstein; sound, Hal Watkins, Aaron
Rochin, Lyle Burbridge, Harry W. Tetrick, William L.
McCaughey; cameras, Gene Polito, Ernest Laszlo, Russell
Metty, Ennio Guarnieri, Allan Green; opticals, Robert
Hoag, Jim Liles; editors, Bud Friedgen, David E. Blewitt.

Narrators: Fred Astaire, Bing Crosby, Gene Kelly, Peter
Lawford, Liza Minnelli, Donald O'Connor, Debbie Rey-
nolds, Mickey Rooney, Frank Sinatra, James Stewart,
Elizabeth Taylor.

DISCOGRAPHY

LONG PLAYING ALBUMS

Compiled by T. Allan Taylor

This discography contains details of American releases plus British release details where applicable.

BEST FOOT FORWARD (Original Cast) Cadence No. CLP 24012, April, 1963.
Contents: *Wish I May, Three Men on a Date, Hollywood Story, The Three Bs* (Liza, Kay Cole, Renee Winters). *Every Time, Alive and Kicking, The Guy Who Brought Me, Shady Lady-Bird, Buckle Down Winsocki, You're Lucky, What Do You Think I Am?* (Edmund Gaynes, Liza, Kay Cole, Ronald Walken), *Raving Beauty, Just a Little Joint with a Jukebox* (Liza, Gene Castle, Don Slaton, Paul Charles), *You Are for Loving* (Liza), *Buckle Down Winsocki* (entire company).

LIZA! LIZA! Capitol No. T 2174, December, 1964, (Reissued as MAYBE THIS TIME—Capitol No. ST 11080). British release: (MAYBE THIS TIME) Capitol No. EST 11080, May, 1973.
Contents: *It's Just a Matter of Time, If I Were in Your Shoes, Meantime, Try to Remember, I'm All I've Got, Maybe Soon, Maybe This Time, Don't Ever Leave Me, Travellin' Time, Together Wherever We Go, Blue Moon, If I Knew Him When.*

IT AMAZES ME—Capitol No. T 2271, June, 1965.
Contents: *Wait Till You See Him, My Shining Hour, I Like the Likes of You, Looking at You, I Never Have Seen Snow, Plenty of Time, For Every Man, Lorelei, Shouldn't There be Lightning?, Nobody Knows You.*

FLORA, THE RED MENACE (Original Cast)—RCA Victor No. LOC 1111, July, 1965.
Contents: Overture, Prologue, *Unafraid* (Liza, students), *All I Need (Is One Good Break)* (Liza), *Not Every Day of the Week* (Liza, Bob Dishy), *Sign Here* (Dishy, Liza), *The Flame, Palomino Pal, A Quiet Thing* (Liza), *Hello Waves* (Dishy,

Liza), *Dear Love* (Liza), *Express Yourself, Knock Knock, Sing Happy* (Liza), *You Are You* (Liza, Joe E. Marks, company).

JUDY GARLAND AND LIZA MINNELLI: 'LIVE' AT THE LONDON PALLADIUM—Capitol No. WBO 2295, October, 1965 (Reissued as a single LP, Capitol No. SWBO 2295, Spring, 1973). British release: Capitol No. EST 11191, September, 1973.

Contents: Overture, *The Man that Got Away, The Travellin' Life* (Liza), *Gypsy in My Soul* (Liza), *Hello, Dolly!* (duet), *Together, Wherever We Go* (duet), *We Could Make Such Beautiful Music* (duet), *Bob White* (duet), *Hooray for Love* (duet), *After You're Gone, By Myself* (Liza), *S'Wonderful, How about You?* (duet), *Lover, Come Back to Me* (Liza), *You and the Night and the Music, It All Depends on You* (duet), *Who's Sorry Now?* (Liza), *Smile, How Could You Believe Me When I Said I Love You, When You Know I've Been a Liar All My Life* (Liza), *What Now My Love, Take Me Along* (Liza), *If I Could Be with You* (Liza), *Tea for Two* (Liza), *Who* (Liza), *They Can't Take that Away from Me* (Liza), *By Myself* (Liza), *Mammy* (Liza), *Make Someone Happy, Pass that Peace Pipe* (Liza), *The Music that Makes Me Dance, When the Saints Go Marching In* (duet), *He's Got the Whole World in His Hands* (duet), *Never Will I Marry, Swanee* (duet), *Chicago* (duet), *Over the Rainbow, San Francisco* (duet).

THERE IS A TIME—Capitol No. T 2448, December, 1966.

Contents: *I Who Have Nothing, M'Lord, Watch What Happens, One of Those Songs, Days of the Waltz, Ay Mariete, Love at Last, Stairway to Paradise, See the Old Man, Parisians.*

THE DANGEROUS CHRISTMAS OF LITTLE RED RIDING HOOD (TV Cast Album)—ABC No. 536, January, 1966.

Contents: Overture, *We wish the World a Happy Yule, My Red Riding Hood* (Liza), *Snubbed, Woodsman's Serenade, Granny's Gulch, Along the Way, I'm Naïve* (Liza, Cyril Ritchard), *Red Riding Hood Improvisation* (ballet), *We're Gonna How, Ding-a-Ling* (Liza, Ritchard), *Poor House* (ballet), *Granny* (Liza, Ritchard), Finale (all).

LIZA MINNELLI—A & M No. 141, May, 1968.

Contents: *Debutante's Ball, Happyland, Look of Love, Butterfly*

McHeart, Waltzing for My Friend, Married, You'd Better Sit Down, Kids, So Long Dad, Nor No One, My Mammy, Happy Time.

COME SATURDAY MORNING—A & M No. SP 4164, April, 1970.

Contents: *Come Saturday Morning, Raggedy Ann and Raggedy Andy, Leavin' on a Jet Plane, Wailing of the Willow, Nevertheless, Wherefore and Why, Love Story, On a Slow Boat to China, Don't Let Me Lose This Dream, Simon, MacArthur Park, Didn't We.*

NEW FEELIN'—A & M No. SP 4272, December, 1970. British release: A & M No. LB 51033, April, 1972.

Contents: *Love for Sale, Stormy Weather, Come Rain or Come Shine, Lazy Bones, Can't Help Lovin' that Man of Mine, (I Wonder Where My) Easy Rider's Gone, The Man I Love, How Long Has This Been Goin' On?, God Bless the Child, Maybe This Time.*

CABARET (Sound Track)—ABC No. DS 752, April, 1972. British release: Anchor No. ABCL 5019, May, 1972.

Contents: *Willkommen, Mein Herr* (Liza), *Two Ladies* (Joel Grey, Liza, Kit-Kat Girls), *Maybe This Time* (Liza), *Sitting Pretty, Tiller Girls, Money, Money, Money,* (Liza, Grey), *Heiraten, If You Could See Her Through My Eyes, Tomorrow Belongs to Me, Cabaret* (Liza), finale.

LIZA MINNELLI 'LIVE' AT THE OLYMPIA— A & M No. SP 4345, July, 1972. British release: A & M No. LS 64345, June, 1972.

Contents: *Everybody's Talkin', Good Morning Starshine, God Bless the Child, Liza with a Z, Married, You'd Better Sit Down, Kids, Nous On S'Aimera, I Will Wait for You, There Is a Time, My Mammy, Everybody Loves My Baby, Cabaret.*

LIZA WITH A Z (TV Show Sound Track)—Columbia No. KC 31762, November, 1972. British release: CBS No. 65212, March, 1973.

Contents: *Yes, God Bless the Child, Liza with a Z, It Was a Good Time, I Gotcha, Ring Them Bells, Son of a Preacher Man, Bye Bye Blackbird, You've Let Yourself Go, My Mammy, Will-*

kommen, Married, Money, Money, Money, Maybe This Time, Cabaret.

THE LIZA MINNELLI FOURSIDER—A & M No. SP 3524, February, 1973. (Reissue compilation). British release: A & M No. AMLC 4003, August, 1973, with the deletion of *Good Morning Starshine* and the addition of *The Look of Love, On a Slow Boat to China, The Wailing of the Willow, Don't Let Me Lose This Dream, Stormy Weather,* and *Can't Help Loving Dat Man.* LP entitled PORTRAIT OF LIZA MINNELLI in Britain.

Contents: *Everybody's Talkin, Good Morning Starshine, Liza with a Z, I Will Wait for You, Cabaret, The Man I Love, Love Story, Married, You'd Better Sit Down, Kids, Leavin' on a Jet Plane, Come Saturday Morning, Nevertheless (I'm in Love with You), Lazy Bones, Come Rain or Come Shine, My Mammy, Waiting for My Friend, MacArthur Park, Didn't We, Maybe This Time, God Bless the Child.*

THE SINGER—Columbia No. KC 32149, May, 1973. British release: CBS No. 6555, May, 1973.

Contents: *I Believe in Music, Use Me, I'd Love You to Want Me, Oh, Babe, What Would You Say?, You're So Vain, Where Is the Love, The Singer, Don't Let Me Be Lonely Tonight, Dancing in the Moonlight, You Are the Sunshine of My Life, Baby Don't Get Hooked on Me.*

MUSCLE OF LOVE—Warner Bros No. S 2748, January, 1974. British release: Warner Bros No. K 56018, December, 1973.

On this Alice Cooper album, Liza performed back-up vocals on two selections: *Teenage Lament '74, Man with Golden Gun.*

LIZA AT THE WINTER GARDEN—Columbia No. TC 32854, May, 1974. British release: CBS No. 69075, May, 1973.

Contents: Overture, *If You Could Read My Mind, Come Back to Me, Shine on Harvest Moon, Exactly Like Me, The Circle, More than You Know, I'm One of the Smart Ones, Natural Man, I Can See Clearly Now, And I In My Chair, There Is a Time, A Quiet Thing, Anywhere You Are, I Believe You, You Made Me Love You.*